MIRACLES TODAY

Understanding How God Participates in Our Lives

by Rodney A. Kvamme

Publishing House
St. Louis

Cover photo by Fred Sieb Photography

The Scripture quotations in this publication are from The Holy Bible: NEW IN-
TERNATIONAL VERSION, © 1973, 1978, 1984 by the International Bible So-
ciety. Used by permission.

Passages so indicated are from J. B. Phillips: THE NEW TESTAMENT IN
MODERN ENGLISH, Revised Edition © J. B. Phillips 1958, 1960, 1972. Used
by permission of Macmillan Publishing Company.

Passages marked RSV are from the Revised Standard Version of the Bible,
© 1946, 1952, © 1971, 1973. Used by permission.

Copyright © 1987 Concordia Publishing House
3558 S. Jefferson Avenue, St. Louis, MO 63118-3968
Manufactured in the United States of America

Library of Congress Cataloging in Publication Data

Kvamme, Rodney A.
        Miracles today.

        1. Jesus Christ—Miracles. 2. Forgiveness of sin. I. Title.
BT366.K82   1986   232.9'55   86-11286
ISBN 0-570-04439-1

1 2 3 4 5 6 7 8 9 10 IB 96 95 94 93 92 91 90 89 88 87

Table of Contents ___

1. Miracles—Now You See Them, Now You Don't

Herman was usually a gentle, soft-spoken man. But now he stood in the hallway by the church office, and he was mad. In a clenched fist, knuckles white and arm trembling, he held a letter. "Why did they have to send this to me now?" It was a mimeographed Christmas letter, indiscriminately mailed to everyone on last year's list. It was written by a pastor and included good news about being healed of cancer. The cancer was described as having been the most deadly of all, painful, inoperative, and fast-spreading. Then, in glowing terms, came the story of immediate and complete healing.

The letter was an invitation to join the celebration of thanksgiving. Why didn't it cause Herman to rejoice? Because Herman's wife was in her last days with cancer. He had prayed, too. The whole congregation had prayed. Healing had not come and did not come. The letter had been written in such terms of "success" that it left Herman deeper in the valley of failure and despair. Herman was right about the letter. A simple, short note expressing concern and assuring continued prayer support would have been so much better.

Erv gave up a career in banking to serve in a church-related position that needed filling due to a man's sudden death. It was a job with many heavy responsibilities and demanded daily difficult decisions. Eventually Erv suffered a nervous breakdown. For about three years he hardly conversed beyond the point of words like "Yes," "No," and "I don't know." He needed something to occupy his time and attention, so he became church custodian in the same town where he had been banker. There was great inner turmoil and bitterness toward God. He felt like tearing down signs on the wall of the church that said "Jesus Is Lord!"

A Lay Witness Mission was planned, and Erv had to set up rooms for the meetings. He determined he would not go. But he went to an evening session where small groups met for discussion and prayer. In that group Erv heard his name mentioned in prayer, although the lady herself says she cannot remember mentioning Erv's name. On the next Saturday, just before Easter, the high school youth were rehearsing their part in the Easter service. They were in different parts of the sanctuary, so that their "Announcement of Easter" would bounce around the nave. As Erv sat listening to this, he felt something like a sharp piercing sensation in his chest. From that very moment, his depression left him.

He had been one of the best lay theologians of my acquaintance. Before his mental breakdown he had been reading several theological books. Now, three years later, he returned to the pages where he had left off and finished reading! He was soon speaking and teaching as before.

However, in the same congregation, there is a person who for years has teetered between severe periods of depression and temporary exhilarating "highs" without experiencing the relief and release that have been prayed for by many friends, relatives, and members of the congregation.

Jan was pregnant, but the doctor discovered the presence of two growths feared to be cancerous. They would have to be surgically removed. It would mean a hysterectomy. The doctor was quite sure the fetus had already died, because all attempts to detect a heartbeat had failed. I sat in the sun porch of the hospital the night before the scheduled surgery. The doctor had just come with his special hearing device to listen one last time for the heartbeat and do final checking before the surgery. I sat and prayed, as many had done, while the doctor and Jan's husband were in the room with her. After some time, the doctor came out shaking his head. "Well, prayers have been answered. There is a distinct heartbeat, and I can find no more evidence of those lumps. I've told Jan she may as well go home. We'll call off the surgery."

After the doctor left, we were sitting in the sun porch, rejoicing over the new turn of events. A young nurse, who had not read the doctor's recent entry on the charts, came to complete some more items on her preoperative checklist. Jan said, "Oh, that's all changed. Instead of surgery, I'm going to have a baby." The nurse was somewhat alarmed and insisted on Jan's full cooperation. As Jan continued to calmly clue the nurse in on what had taken place, the nurse grew more alarmed and finally said, as though this would end all discussion, "Well, you've got to have your surgery because you have already had your enema!" She was not convinced until she made a special trip to read the chart.

There were other precarious moments as time went on, but Jan is well, and so is the husky little boy.

Another couple was excited about the prospect of having a child. Prayer for a safe delivery was a daily petition. Everything seemed to be going well. Suddenly, labor started. There was a rush to the hospital, and the baby was born two months premature. Baptism took place, but within 24 hours Heidi ("daughter of God") Dawn ("new and eternal life with God") died from a lung deficiency.

Two men are walking miracles. Vic was crushed by a falling tractor, and his pelvic bones were mashed. There was little hope that he would ever walk again. But Vic is walking and rides horseback more than any cattleman in the area.

Marv's back was broken in a car wreck. Wherever he went, doctors told him to adjust to the fact that he would never get around outside a wheelchair. But he began to walk, first with crutches and then a cane. Already he testified that the accident had resulted in a new peace with God that outweighed the problems and pain. The day he took his first steps without a cane, he came to church so we could kneel at the altar in thanksgiving.

But another, younger man, who also broke his back, has remained in his wheelchair now for several years with no prospect of ever leaving it.

What shall we say about such a mix of miracles and nonmiracles? How can we rejoice with those who are healed, without adding discouragement to those not relieved of their illness, pain, or handicap? Whenever spiritual renewal takes place, there seems to be an increased hunger for the miraculous. This may be because people become more open to the intervention of God in their lives. But while the excitement of miracles grabs center stage, there are hurting people in the wings left with nagging questions and unmet needs.

Is there a bigger view that will hold both the successes and failures? Is there something greater to cling to than firsthand evidence of a miracle in our midst? Are there clues in the Scriptures? Were the miracles of Jesus specific ends in themselves, or were they also avenues of communication for good news to everyone?

I am convinced that the miraculous is still among us. I am also convinced that when a miracle takes place on center stage, or even if it doesn't take place, there is large writing on the back wall that we had better not overlook. That writing includes words like FORGIVENESS and RESTORED. This is the major miracle that every person may experience and celebrate. These same words were written large in connection with all of Jesus' miracles. This is the theme we will pursue: "Restored by Love—The Miracles of Jesus as Forgiveness."

Something to think/talk/pray about

—Can you recall instances of the miraculous in your life or someone else's?

—Do you know anyone who is hurting because there seems to be no relief from a problem or pain?

—Thank God that He has made forgiveness available to you through Jesus.

2. The Miracles of Jesus as Forgiveness (Mark 2:1–12)

A miracle is "an act or happening in the material or physical sphere that apparently departs from the laws of nature or goes beyond what is known concerning these laws." Yet, *miracle* is not a big word in the New Testament. There are three other words used more often. One comes from the same Greek source as our word *dynamite*. It means "act of power" or "mighty act" and draws attention to the *source* of such power or might. In other words, the miracle or mighty act is not separated from the mighty *One* who does the action. The miracles of Jesus were always more than amazing feats. They were testimonies of the presence in the world of One whose power could accomplish these marvelous acts. The other words in the New Testament relating to miracles are *wonders* and *signs*. Since they are always used together, it is evident again that the miracles were meant to do more than simply impress. They did more than solve a problem of a person or the crowd. The miracles wrote or "signed" in capital letters the message that God was at work among His people.

Each person may have a different and favorite way of summarizing that work of God in his life. One may say, "I've been redeemed" or "I'm saved," and revel in the way God has bought him back and brought him back. Another may testify, "I have been made right with God." This celebrates the fact that Jesus has broken down all the barriers. Still another may confess, "I have been baptized," and rest securely in that definite and gracious action of acceptance by the Lord.

My favorite summary is this: "I am forgiven!" *Forgive* is a household word, one that we use to express something that we experience in our everyday relationships with others. It assures us that we are at home and at one with them. *Forgive* has heavy theological content without having the heavy sound of some more complicated words like *justification* or *regeneration*. Webster's unabridged dictionary (second edition) uses four Scripture references to help define this common word. One definition is as follows: "To cease to feel resentment against, on account of wrong committed; to give up claim to requital from or retribution upon (an offender); to absolve; pardon. 'Father, forgive them; for they know not what they do.' Luke 23:34." When I use the word *forgiveness*, I let it carry the heavy cargo of many Biblical concepts such as redemption, atonement, reconciliation. It would be more precise to carry many separate baskets, but I find it less cumbersome to carry one basket even though it contains several theological picnic items.

It is quite possible for us to profane forgiveness. This becomes true if it is exercised in a shallow way that only indulges another person's wrong, or if it is done in resignation or disgust. God's forgiveness, as ours should be, is quite the opposite. His is *true restoration*, so complete that it is *as though the offense had never occurred*. Also, part of God's package of forgiveness includes strength for future improvement. God could rightfully be forgive*less*, but by pure grace He has opted to be a God of forgive*ness*.

To say that there is a connection between miracles and forgiveness is not anything original. If there is anything original in our investigation of the miracles, it will be to see that forgiveness is the thread that runs through all the miracle accounts. In other words, whenever a miracle takes place, the miracle is not the big thing. Forgiveness is the big thing. Jesus' central mission was not to fill every stomach (feeding 5,000), to bring perfect weather conditions to the world (calming the storm), or to heal every sickness. He was never unconcerned about the very down-to-earth problems and needs of man, but forgiveness was His primary business.

He was on an errand of redemption, restoration, reconciliation. His mission was a ministry of the Word, which was accompanied by signs and wonders. It was not a ministry of miracles accompanied by some preaching. When He went into synagogues, His purpose was to teach, although He also performed some miracles in the synagogues: "They went to Capernaum, and when the Sabbath came, Jesus went into the synagogue and began to teach" (Mark 1:21). When He determined to go to certain towns or sections of the country, it was in order that He might *preach* there: "Jesus replied, 'Let us go somewhere else—to the nearby villages—so I can preach there also. That is why I have come' " (Mark 1:38). His preaching was often an occasion for miracles, but He did not set up shop and perform miracles so that they might be an occasion for preaching.

This is the situation in Mark 2, where Mark profoundly connects miracle with forgiveness: "A few days later, when Jesus again entered Capernaum, the people heard that he had come home. So many gathered that there was no room left, not even outside the door, and he preached the word to them" (Mark 2:1–2). Preaching was Jesus' main occupation and primary concern when He was with people. So consistent and persistent was He as God's Messenger that the apostle John, closer to Jesus than any other disciple during Jesus' ministry, referred to Jesus as the Word, with a capital W: "In the beginning was the Word, and the Word was with God, and the Word was God. . . . The Word became flesh and made his dwelling among us" (John 1:1 and 14). Phillips' translation brings this out in an interesting way: "At the beginning God expressed himself. That personal expression, that word, was with God and was God. . . . So the word of God became a human being and lived among us."

In a way, Jesus' miracles complicated His preaching ministry. There is the old expression: "What you do speaks so loudly I can't hear what you say." Jesus was aware that this could happen and that His miracles could come across so loudly that they would drown out His message about the Kingdom. Mark says that when a leper came to Jesus for healing, Jesus was moved with pity and cleansed him but instructed him to tell no one. In fact, Mark says, "Jesus sent him away at once with a strong warning: 'See that you don't tell this to anyone' " (Mark 1:43–44). This was not false modesty on Jesus' part. He wasn't faking humility when He said He didn't want this miracle noised around. He was serious. He was not sent by God to hang up a shingle that said "Faith healing done here." He wanted His message strengthened and enhanced, but not garbled by signs and wonders. He did not want people coming to Him for the wrong motives, as when the multitude wanted to crown Him their king

11

after He had fed them so well in the wilderness. "Jesus, knowing that they intended to come and make him king by force, withdrew again to a mountain by himself" (John 6:15).

But the leper didn't keep quiet. Mark says: "Instead he went out and began to talk freely, spreading the news. As a result, Jesus could no longer enter a town openly but stayed outside in lonely places. Yet the people still came to him from everywhere" (1:45). It wasn't long after Jesus got to Capernaum that four men knew He was in town and came carrying their crippled buddy to Jesus (Mark 2:3–5). They certainly had faith in Jesus. You don't tear up a roof to get to a person in whom you do not believe. Jesus saw their faith, Mark says.

In nearly every miracle account a faith relationship is evident, spoken or unspoken. But it is not in the form of a quotation from the Catechism, and it is hardly ever neatly expressed and well phrased. Sometimes it is a cry of frustration, like that of blind Bartimaeus: "When he heard that it was Jesus of Nazareth, he began to shout, 'Jesus, Son of David, have mercy on me!' " (Mark 10:47). Sometimes it springs from fear, as with the disciples in the capsizing boat: "The disciples went and woke him, saying, 'Lord, save us! We're going to drown!' " (Matt. 8:25). It may be an unspoken need of the multitude in the wilderness: "When Jesus looked up and saw a great crowd coming toward him, he said to Philip, 'Where shall we buy bread for these people to eat?' " (John 6:5).

With the four men, faith was expressed in their act of getting their friend to Jesus one way or another. Yet there was this difference. With the men the *miracle* was the greatest thing, while with Jesus the miracle was subordinate to forgiveness. Jesus' first words to the paralytic were not, "Be healed" but "Son, your sins are forgiven" (Mark 2:5). Mark doesn't indicate what the first reaction of the men was. I would guess that on the inside they were thinking, "Lord, that's not why we came!" But they didn't get a chance to express themselves. The scribes were stirred to action by Jesus' words. They had been sitting puzzled by the words and deeds of this Jesus. Now suddenly they had a case against Him. They now had a calling to defend God against this Jesus, who talked as though He had power to forgive sin. These scribes would ordinarily have been correct. Forgiveness of sin is God's prerogative. There was only one chance in all the world that these scribes would be wrong to make a case of this—

but this was the one time. The Son of Man *did* have authority on earth to forgive sins, and they were about to have this forgiveness visualized in the healing of the paralytic.

"[Jesus said,] 'Which is the easier: to say to the paralytic, "Your sins are forgiven," or to say "Get up, take up your mat and walk"?' " (Mark 2:9). I think we would agree that "Your sins are forgiven" would be the hardest for anyone to disprove. But to say "Rise and walk" to a cripple would open you up to a real chance of being discredited. However, were the cripple to rise and walk as directed, who would then dare question Jesus' power when He pronounced the man's sins forgiven? This was precisely Jesus' point—"That you may know that the Son of Man has authority on earth to forgive sins"(Mark 2:10)—and then comes the command of healing, the momentary suspense, the quivering of shriveled limbs, the astonishing action of the man getting up and, after being a burden for years, picking up the burden of his own pallet and making his exit from the crowd, who stand stunned and amazed.

We have in this miracle a clear case of forgiveness in action, forgiveness acted out in the physical restoration of a crippled body. There is the possibility that the crippling came as a result of the man's own misbehavior, which may have been known by the crowd or at least by the four men who brought him. If so, the relationship between forgiveness and healing is all the more impressive.

In this miracle account the relationship between miracle and forgiveness is plain. Can we find this in Jesus' other miracles? We shall see.

Before we leave this text, however, there is one more point I want to make. There is a way this miracle can help you and me today in our assurance of God's forgiveness toward us. Today there are those who turn things around from what I have said. I have not discounted the miracle at all. In fact, I would not have anything to say if I discounted the authenticity of miracles. But miracles are still second to forgiveness. Miracles are temporary wonders. This cripple did not live forever on the basis of his physical healing. He is not living today. He got sick and died. Even Lazarus, who was raised from the dead, died again, and the grave now holds him until the final resurrection. Miracles are temporary, but forgiveness leads to eternal life. Forgiveness has a permanence that even miracles cannot provide, and the paralytic received the gift of forgiveness before his healing. Forgiveness was his even if he had lain crippled the rest of his life. Jesus had spoken forgiveness to him, and that forgiveness was not dependent on the man's getting up and walking. A miracle had already taken place in this man's life before the miracle of his healing. He had been forgiven. Unless you doubt Jesus' words, you would have to agree that this was so. Even if the man had never been able to walk, his life would have shown that something had happened. Forgiveness itself is a miracle, and people who have been spiritual cripples, bent over with anguish, uptight on the inside with guilt, shaken by uncertainty of God's love, are renewed and restored when Jesus' words of forgiveness come and they know that He is speaking to them.

There are people today with heavy loads. It might be a physical ailment or a mental strain. It might be just an unsettled feeling you can't describe. Know that Jesus wants you to hear His words: "My son, my daughter, your sins are forgiven." That is His gift to you now, only for the asking—even without the asking, because He already knows your need. The miracle of forgiveness is available to you. God will not hold you accountable for your sins—He frees you in Jesus' name. This freedom will make its mark in your life. You operate differently as a forgiven child of His. Your circumstances may change for the better. If they do, thank God. They may not change at all, but you will be better equipped to handle them. Thank God for this, too. You do not have to come to Him equipped to receive forgiveness. He equips you by speaking His forgiveness to you, which empowers you to walk taller in this world than you have ever walked before, to carry more burdens, yours and those of others, and to accomplish more tasks while giving Him the glory.

There are some miracles you may, or may not, experience in your life. But the miracle of forgiveness is one God does not want you to miss. Should anyone ask whether you have experienced a miracle, answer, "Yes, I have been forgiven." Don't feel inadequate because you are no "healer." You can be a "forgiveness-bringer," which makes you a miracle worker in the finest sense of the word.

Something to think/talk/pray about

—What is your favorite way of summarizing the work of God in your life?

—God's forgiveness is so complete that it is as though the offense had never occurred. Thank Him for that, and ask Him to help you to forgive some specific person who has offended you.

—"The Good News, not great miracles, was Jesus' main interest." How do you react to this statement?

—Even miracles are temporary. How might it be encouraging to remember this?

—If you could have a reputation as a "healer" or as a "forgiveness-bringer," which would you choose and why?

3. Forgiveness in the Flesh (the Incarnation) ___

Under the theme "The Miracles of Jesus as Forgiveness" we considered the encounter of Jesus with the paralytic, to whom Jesus first spoke the forgiveness of sins and whom He then healed physically as evidence of His power to forgive. We are now ready to test this thesis on another miracle. Usually the miracles that we investigate will concern things that Jesus did. But in this chapter the miracle we consider is not something that He did, but rather what He was. Jesus Himself was a miracle. We said that a miracle is "an act or happening in the material or physical sphere that apparently departs from the laws of nature or goes beyond what is known concerning these laws." Jesus' conception was a miracle. We call it the Incarnation, God becoming incarnate, God coming to earth "in the flesh."

The account of creation in Genesis tells of how God first began the business of human life on the earth. He molded man out of the dust, "breathed into his nostrils the breath of life, and the man became a living being" (Gen. 2:7). After creating male and female, God established the re-creation of life through the coming together of man and woman in the flesh. This means that in a very real way you and I have our existence, our "enfleshment," by the courtesy and command of God.

But when Jesus was born, God took His prerogative as Creator and established His own unique way of entering this physical life. The Incarnation identified Jesus with both man and God. In Jesus' birth, God did not deny His own design of entering earthly life—Jesus was born of a woman. But God did intervene uniquely in a way that stressed His special involvement in Christ's coming. "The virgin will be with child and will give birth to a son" (Is. 7:14). The angel said to Mary: "The Holy Spirit will come upon you, and the power of the Most High will overshadow you. So the holy one to be born will be called the Son of God" (Luke 1:35).

Jesus' birth was a miracle. Even more, it was a miracle of forgiveness. His incarnation was forgiveness in the flesh. When an angel spoke to Joseph in a dream, the message included instructions about the name of the child: "You are to give him the name Jesus, for he will save his people from their sins" (Matt. 1:21). The name Jesus is a form of the original Hebrew name Joshua, which means "Jehovah will save" or "Jehovah is salvation." It would make an interesting study to follow the parallel suggested by early church fathers between Joshua of the Old Testament and Jesus, that is, how Joshua led the old Israel through the waters of the Jordan into the Promised Land as compared with Jesus leading the new Israel, his church, through the waters of Baptism into the promised kingdom of heaven.

Matthew mentions another name that would apply to Jesus. This was the name Emmanuel, which means "God with us" (Matt. 1:23). Forgiveness is intimately connected with this name, too. After the fall of man into sin, man became uncomfortable in the presence of God. The writer of Genesis puts it this way: "The man and his wife heard the sound of the Lord God as he was walking in the garden in the cool of the day, and they hid from the Lord God among the trees of the garden" (Gen. 3:8). Ever since, people have tended to be uncomfortable in the presence of God. The first impulse is to seek to hide from Him, or come into His presence with our guard up, ready to make as good a defense of ourselves as possible. But in Jesus Christ, God chose to walk once again with His people, this time in a garden of weeds, a world of sin. He came calling them again to come out of hiding, be reconciled, walk with Him, forgiven and at peace.

The birth of Jesus was God's offer of a new beginning, and this is precisely one meaning of forgiveness—the offer of a new beginning. This offer of a new beginning can be seen most clearly as we continue to contrast the two scenes of Jesus' birth and the fall of man. The birth of Jesus was an act of forgiveness on God's part.

Forgiveness of Man's Fallen State

It was forgiveness of man's fallen state. How much simpler it would have been for God to discard His fallen world and start over. This would have been a simple matter for God, except for one thing—His love. Love complicated the issue for God. It still does. God never has delighted in the death or destruction of the wicked. Salvation, not destruction, is His joy.

Our washer once flooded the basement, and there was no drain in the basement. There was about an inch of water all over the floor. Lots of things got soaked. Among them were two stuffed toys, a big dog named Sam and a little donkey named Donkey. They were both well worn, and the stuffing was falling out. Now they were soaked and stained and soon started to smell very musty. The painful decision was made that they had to be thrown away. It was a sad trip to the dump, though they were given the honor befitting a flag or a Bible. They were thrown into a fire so they would not just lie around and rot. But there was no happiness connected with their destruction.

There was another favorite stuffed toy at our house. He was Smokey the Bear. Smokey was coming apart at the seams and looked quite hopeless, too; but he had escaped the flood, and love prevailed. The combination was a persistent little boy, a determined mother, and a bag of new foam stuffing. The salvage project was a success. Smokey never looked so good and was never loved more. Real joy comes from salvation, not destruction. The conception and birth of Jesus the Savior was God coming to earth on an errand of salvation, propelled by a willingness to forgive and a determination to redeem.

Recapturing an Original Intent

The birth of Christ was forgiveness in the sense of being an offer of a new beginning by recapturing the original intent for the first Adam to be a man after God's heart. God had loved enough in the beginning to want to be loved in return. He chose not to create people in such a way that they had no other option but to love Him. This would not have been love or fellowship. Love means something only when it is freely given. So man was given the option to love God or rebel against Him. Man voted for rebellion. The choice was man's to make, but the consequences were set. Disobedience shut man out from all the good that God had planned for His people. What was lost by the first Adam would be regained by Jesus, the second Adam. Paul makes this clear in his letter to the Romans: "Just as the result of one trespass was condemnation for all men, so also the result of one act of righteousness was justification that brings life for all men. For

18

just as through the disobedience of the one man the many were made sinners, so also through the obedience of the one man the many will be made righteous" (Rom. 5:18–19).

Vision of True Manhood Restored

Besides this recapturing of the original relationship of obedience and blessing, the birth of Christ was forgiveness in that the vision of true manhood in all its dimensions was flashed again across the face of the earth. God desired more than obedience for the sake of obedience alone. He knew that abundant life could be tasted by people only when they were in a proper stance to receive it. Jesus was not true man simply because He was cut after our pattern and felt pain, hunger, sorrow, temptation, fatigue, and other human emotions. He was true man because He was cut after *God's* pattern for manhood and sought love, truth, beauty, and justice along paths that others neither dreamed of traveling nor dared to. Again, the apostle Paul compares Jesus and the first Adam and uses terms that hint of the false and faulty goals and achievements of Adam over against the true and attained goals and achievements of Jesus. Paul uses the frail word "dust" in referring to Adam. He uses the word "heaven" in reference to Jesus. "The first man was from the earth, a man of dust; the second man is from heaven. As was the man of dust, so are those who are of the dust; and as is the man of heaven, so are those who are of heaven. Just as we have borne the image of the man of dust, we shall also bear the image of the man of heaven" (1 Cor. 15:47–49 RSV). The birth of Christ was forgiveness, a new beginning, holding out once more the opportunity for men to reach the full stature of true sons of God.

God Saying "Good" Again

Finally, the Incarnation was a new beginning because it was God saying again of something in this world—"Good." The book of Genesis testifies that God gave final inspection to what He had created, and it all passed inspection. Over and over the phrase is repeated—"God saw that it was good. . . . And God saw that it was good. . . . God saw all that he had made, and it was very good" (Gen. 1:12, 18, 31). Not for long could He say that about His world. By the time of Noah the Bible says: "The Lord saw how great man's wickedness on the earth had become, and that every inclination of the thoughts of his heart was only evil all the time. The Lord was grieved that he had made man on the earth, and his heart was filled with pain" (Gen. 6:5–6). The night when Jesus was born marked a new beginning for the world, and God sent His angels down to earth to sing about it. He said "Good" again when Jesus was a grown man and about to begin His years of ministry. At His baptism came the announcement from heaven that echoed the Creator's pronouncement of "Good" in the beginning—"As soon as Jesus was baptized, he went up out of the water. At that moment heaven was opened, and he saw the Spirit of God descending like a dove and lighting on him. And a voice from heaven said, 'This is my Son, whom I love; with him I am well pleased' " (Matt. 3:16–17). In these words was the divine optimism that a lost world could be regained and a straying people recalled to their original purpose and life with God.

The birth of Jesus Christ was forgiveness in action, forgiveness incarnate, forgiveness in the flesh. The miracle of Christmas Day made everyday forgiveness possible.

One experience of everyday forgiveness in the flesh has lingered in my memory for over 10 years. Our family was out for a walk. The exact location is still clear in my mind—it happened while we were going past a small grocery store. My youngest son, then a preschooler, was holding my hand. I don't recall what I had done, but I do remember that I had to admit being wrong about something and asked my family to forgive me. Just at that point my boy squeezed my hand. It was his absolution, and the sense of that incarnate forgiveness is still vivid and real.

Forgiveness as a new beginning characterizes everyday life with Jesus, too. Apart from Him, I would have to carry a big bag of garbage representing all my sins, shortcomings, failures. I would set it off my back at night, put it in the corner, but be faced by it the first thing in the morning. I would go over to the garbage and begin hoisting it up in order to hump under the load for one more day. But then Jesus intercepts me and says, "Kvamme, what do you think the cross was all about? I hung there to carry your sins so that you wouldn't have to. Now leave that bag of garbage with Me, and go into the new day. I give you the gift of a fresh start, a new beginning." I respond, "Oh, thanks, Lord, that's what I have needed." As I go off to the new day, Jesus shouts after me, "Hey, don't forget this when you meet others throughout the day. They may also be under heavy loads, so don't add to their burdens by putting on any complaints or bitterness. Pass My gift on to them. If you have needed the fresh start of My forgiveness, you may be sure that others need it just as badly." And so forgiveness in the flesh began at the Incarnation, but it continues in the everyday lives of Christ's people.

Something to think/talk/pray about

—Jesus not only *did* miracles; but *was* a miracle. Explain this in your own words.
—Can you think of a special forgiveness-event that has taken place among your family or friends?
—The gift of a fresh start—thank God for it and think of people who need this gift from you.

4. Nature's Response to Forgiveness (Nature Miracles)

God said, "Let us make man in our image, in our like-
ness, and let them rule over the fish of the sea and the
birds of the air, over the livestock, over all the earth,
and over all the creatures that move along the ground."
So God created man in his own image, in the image of
God he created him; male and female he created them.
God blessed them and said to them, "Be fruitful and
increase in number; fill the earth and subdue it. Rule
over the fish of the sea and the birds of the air and over
every living creature that moves on the ground." Then
God said, "I give you every seed-bearing plant on the
face of the whole earth and every tree that has fruit with
seed in it. They will be yours for food" (Gen. 1:26–29).

So it was in the beginning. God made the earth, then man.
Then He proceeded to put the whole earth at man's disposal and
said, "All that I have stands ready to respond to your needs."
The man was to till and keep a garden in which there was everything to satisfy him. Only one tree was left beyond his reach. He
grabbed for that one tree and, in doing so, let all the rest of God's
creation slip from his grasp.

Then came the curse. This was not so much an act of God
getting even with man for his disobedience. Rather, to use a
phrase of Harley Swiggum, author of the Bethel Series, the curse
was a "pronouncement of the inevitable." As man acted in proud,
selfish, and ungrateful ways, he would continue to turn into curses
what God had first intended to be blessings. "To Adam he [God]

22

said, 'Because you listened to your wife and ate from the tree about which I commanded you, "You must not eat of it," cursed is the ground because of you; through painful toil you will eat of it all the days of your life. It will produce thorns and thistles for you, and you will eat the plants of the field. By the sweat of your brow you will eat your food until you return to the ground, since from it you were taken; for dust you are and to dust you will return' " (Gen. 3:17–19).

Yet there always has remained a residue of longing to return to Paradise. Paul says the whole earth shares this longing. "The creation waits in eager expectation for the sons of God to be revealed. For the creation was subjected to frustration, not by its own choice, but by the will of the one who subjected it, in hope that the creation itself will be liberated from its bondage to decay and brought into the glorious freedom of the children of God" (Rom. 8:19–21). He goes on to say that the whole creation is groaning in travail in its anxiety to see the curse lifted and man once again reconciled to nature, with all traces of rebellion, antagonism, competition, warring, and opposition removed.

The nature miracles of Jesus are a sign that God is at work in the world to bring about this reconciliation. Since the curse of the ground, the battle has raged as men seek to force the physical world to give up and produce what is necessary for his needs. In justice, God allowed the inevitable result of disobedience to show itself in the return of the earth to a chaotic state. In loving forgiveness, however, God has determined to bring all things ultimately back together again through His Son. In the nature miracles of Jesus we see the forgiveness of the curse of the ground, with the result that earth responds perfectly to the needs of man. To put it in words of Genesis, Jesus exhibits man with perfect dominion over all the things of the earth.

First let's look at some miracles relating to man's need for food, an area where man is dependent on physical creation. At the wedding in Cana, Jesus turned water into wine (John 2:1–11). John says this was the first of Jesus' signs. There was plenty of water available, but wine was used at the wedding, and, because of someone's oversight, not enough wine had been provided for the celebration. Jesus does not even speak words that induce the miracle. He simply has the servants fill the jars with water, which they had, and then serve the guests. But when they served it, it was wine, which they needed. The elements reacted to the very desire or need of man, without the toil and sweat mentioned in the Genesis curse. The curse of the ground was forgiven.

The feeding of the multitude in the wilderness is in the same category. The accounts of feeding the 5,000 (Mark 6:30–44; Matt. 14:19–21; Luke 9:10–17; John 6:5–14) and of feeding the 4,000 (Mark 8:1–9; Matt. 15:32–38) are quite similar in description. With the 5,000, the biggest apprehension seemed to be finances. The disciples couldn't imagine going into town and spending the amount of money it would take to feed such a multitude. With the 4,000, the greatest concern of Jesus was distance. They were remote from any towns, and the crowd had been in the wilderness with Him for three days. He feared that some would faint going back to their cities if they didn't have something to eat first. Except for these different concerns, the circumstances were about the same. They were in a barren section of country that typified the curse of the ground. There were no fruit trees or berry bushes or grain crops that could be used for food. The only source was the leftovers from previous meals. As Jesus multiplied this meager supply, the result was the same as if He had created before them a lake with fish eager to be caught and a field of grain ripe and ready for harvest. The miracle was a forgiveness of the curse of the ground, and these earthly elements multiplied and volunteered their nourishment to meet men's needs.

Did you notice that the words of Genesis about dominion began with the unlikely thought of man ruling over the fish of the sea? Any fisherman will testify that usually fish are a good example of the curse of the ground. That is, they are not exactly eager to jump into the boat of the fisherman or toward the man on shore who stands holding a frying pan instead of a fish pole! In the days of Jesus, the net was the fisherman's principal tool. On one particular night Simon had had no luck at all (Luke 5:1–11). Jesus came by when Simon was washing his nets. He asked Simon to take Him out on the lake in his boat, and then to put his net in the water for a catch. Simon said, "Master, we've worked hard all night and haven't caught anything." It was his way of saying, "It's no use, Lord." But he did obey—and got the surprise of his life. His net filled with fish, as did the boat, and his partners' boat. The curse had lifted. Instead of toiling for nothing, the result of their labor was food in abundance. The incident had a strange effect on Peter. It convicted him of his sin. "Go away from me, Lord; I am a sinful man!" It seems like a strange response, yet not so strange. Things as they were meant to be, that is, nature in perfect response to Jesus, confronted Peter with all that he had failed to be, and he confessed his sin. The apostle John records another great catch of fish (John 21:4–6). This was directed by Jesus after He had risen from the dead. The first time Peter had felt like running *from* Jesus. This time he raced *toward* Jesus, even when it meant jumping out of the boat and swimming to shore because it was faster. He couldn't wait to get to his risen, forgiving Lord, whom he had denied. Another "fish story" involving Jesus and Peter is told by Matthew (17:24–27). At best Peter had hoped to make a living by catching and selling fish. But in this incident nature is so subservient to men's needs that a fish is hooked and inside the mouth of the fish is a shekel to pay taxes!

The miracle of the fig tree (Mark 11:12–14; Matt. 21:18–22) is a reverse of the ordinary. Jesus was hungry. As He walked along, He saw this fig tree. It had leaves, and this was the sign that there should also be figs on it. There were none. Jesus cursed the tree, and it died. Instead of forgiveness of the curse, the curse seemed enacted and reinforced. Although it therefore doesn't seem connected to forgiveness, Jesus connects it to exactly that as He discusses it with Peter. Jesus uses it to teach a lesson concerning faith, prayer, and forgiveness (Mark 11:20–26). He told Peter that, with faith, mountains could be moved. Therefore anything asked in believing prayer will be given. But when you pray, be sure to forgive others and also know God's forgiveness, so that all barriers between you and God and you and other people are down. Forgiveness is the backdrop against which all things are possible.

We have mostly discussed miracles relating to the need for food. The other major nature miracles concern transportation, if we can put it in such common untheological language. The setting of the first pits man against the sea (Matt. 8:23–27). The disciples were in a boat. Waves were about to capsize it. They were all terrified, but Jesus was asleep. When they woke Him, it is funny how nonchalant He was in asking what they were afraid of . . . (they were afraid of losing their lives, that's what they were afraid of!). The water was a potential killer as men sought to travel over it. Here was part of nature that man could not tame but that often rose up in fury against him. As Jesus spoke His "Peace, be still," the curse of the elements was forgiven, and the winds and waves responded like obedient children and quieted down. "What kind of man is this?" they asked. The answer? A true man of God with perfect power to subdue the earth and make it yield to His needs. So the curse lifted. The winds and waves ceased their rebellions and became submissive to the needs of men.

Other accounts (Mark 6:45–51; Matt. 14:22–33; John 6:16–21) tell of Jesus walking on the water and Peter's attempt to do the same. What can we say of this? Either the story is not true and didn't happen at all, or else the curse involving man and the elements was lifted, forgiven. Jesus traveled by land, sea, and air without the assistance of boat or airplane. We could dispense with this by simply saying that He was God, so He could do anything. But it seems more correct to say that He was operating as man in perfect relationship to God and with perfect God-given dominion over the earth. I say this seems more correct since, in the account of walking on the water, Peter does the same thing as Jesus, at least for a short time, and this does not mean that Peter had any divinity of his own to accomplish the trick. As long as Peter was in that perfect faith-relationship, he walked without sinking. When he was overcome again by his human and earthly surroundings, his apprehension caused him to sink. The explanation does not lie in saying that the water was suddenly made more dense than the ground so that it supported their weight. Here was a state of forgiveness, a lifting of the curse of the ground, a taking away of that which caused water to be a problem to man rather than a help. When Jesus desired to walk to the other side of the lake, it was simply more to His interest to walk across on the water than to walk the long distance around on the land. At that point the water was subject to Him in the need He had for it.

There are other brief references that picture elements in nature ready to respond to man's needs. Examples of these are Jesus' words that mountains (Mark 11:23; Matt. 17:20) and trees (Luke 17:6) will obey commands uttered in faith. And in speaking of the last days, He indicated that sun, moon, stars, and seas will take other than their usual roles to trumpet His final coming (Luke 21:25). Man is never given the right to use his dominion indiscriminately or for vengeance, however. When some Samaritans did not respond properly to Jesus, the disciples were ready to call down fire from heaven, but Jesus rebuked them (Luke 9:54–55).

The only nature miracle referring to creatures other than fish deals with serpents. In Mark 16:18 Jesus said that one of the signs that would accompany those who believe would be that they will pick up deadly serpents. This is in stark contrast to the fall of man, where the serpent overpowered Adam and Eve. Now, in the relationship of faith and forgiveness, the serpent would be powerless against the believer. Some sects have misinterpreted this to the point where handling snakes has become a test to see if you are a Christian. Jesus never said this. Such an interpretation would be as ridiculous as saying a Christian should drink glycerine to test his faith because Jesus said in that same part of Mark: "When they drink deadly poison, it will not hurt them at all."

Because Jesus knew of people's tendency to misunderstand or misuse His promises, He said in Luke 10:19–20, "I have given you authority to trample on snakes and scorpions, and to overcome all the power of the enemy; nothing will harm you." Here He clearly ties this power to the reminder of victory over that old serpent, the devil. But Jesus went on: "However, do not rejoice that the spirits submit to you, but rejoice that your names are written in heaven." In the apostle John's vision of heaven, it is the Lamb that opens the Book of Life while the song of praise is sung: "You are worthy to take the scroll and to open its seals, because you were slain, and with your blood you purchased men for God from every tribe and language and people and nation" (Rev. 5:9). The Who's Who in God's Book of Life is not based on who has performed mighty works, but on who has believed the message of *God's* mighty works in Christ and has received forgiveness and redemption in Him.

In the nature miracles we have seen Jesus operating in areas where the curse of the natural world was temporarily lifted or suspended. Nature's response to forgiveness was immediate and complete. If only our response to God's forgiveness would be the same!

I wish I were in a position to host two conferences. One would gather theologians and ecologists. The nature miracles would be the basic agenda. A study would revolve around Jesus' attitude and actions toward the natural world. He had such great respect and such great expectations. We could learn good ecological habits from Him. We tend to form pictures in our minds of "man battling the elements." How about, instead of that, encouraging a repentant attitude of man toward all of nature? After all, it was the disobedience of the creatures of consciousness (people) that carried along all the consciousless creatures and creation on the sad journey from God's "Good" to His "Cursed." The consciousless still seem to sense the divine in awesome ways. Perhaps serpents have at times detected the change in attitude and perspective among the new creatures in Christ and have therefore refrained from venomous attack upon them. There was a fourth presence, like the Son of God, in the fiery furnace with Shadrach, Meschach, and Abednego, and the fire didn't harm them. The lions spared Daniel because they were in the presence of an angelic representative of the Lord. In Jesus you find a caring person speaking "Peace" to a stormy wind as though it were a traumatized child who needed soothing. Through Jesus, Christians are inheritors of an exemplary concern for and appreciation of the natural world.

The second conference would bring together theologians and anthropologists. Since this would be my own mythical meeting, I would set the agenda and determine the results! There would be an opening ceremony that would mark the end of the search for the missing link. In its stead there would be a new appreciation of the importance of the serpent in human affairs. The Bible hints that the serpent was at the head of its class among creatures. Of all the animals, people may have felt the greatest kinship to the serpent, and that may well be why it was a reasonable choice as an instrument of Satan in his tempting plan—for who would suspect a friend of leading you astray! After the Fall and the curse, the serpent was drastically changed (Gen. 3:14). Therefore the anthropologists would search for references to serpents in ancient literature, etc. Attention would focus on the king cobra.

We won't all be invited to the conferences! They may never be convened. Nevertheless, we may all learn from Jesus' miracles a respect and expectation regarding the world of nature—instead of fear, disregard, or contempt. We may even learn to exercise an attitude of repentance and forgiveness toward it.

The story is told of a drought-stricken area whose citizens agreed to ask the Lord for rain. When they all came together for prayer, only one, a four-year-old girl, brought an umbrella. There are so many areas in which we can learn and grow concerning the nature of things and the things of nature—in a contentment with things as they are, in a boldness to pray for change, and in the trusting practice of carrying an umbrella.

Something to think/talk/pray about

—Spend some time meditating on your kinship to all living things, especially animals and plants. If possible, find a place where you can look out over a beautiful scene. Maybe just sit and look at a pet or plant in your home. Realize that God's wonderful gift of life is shared by you and by them.

—Close your eyes and imagine that you are in the Garden of Eden. You have an intense feeling of oneness with all living things. Ask God to increase that sense of unity and wonder about His creation, which you share.

5. Dynamic Forgiveness (Healing Miracles) _

It would be presumptuous to think that healing miracles could be treated adequately within the confines of one chapter. There are more than 60 references to healing in the gospels, so this must be an attempt to pull together only some threads that seem to entwine throughout these many references. There are four of these: healing as physical release, healing as fulfillment of prophecy, healing as dynamic forgiveness, and healing as a foretaste of heaven.

Physical Release

First, let us consider healing as physical release. It surely was this. If you discount the validity of miraculous physical healing, you will blunt your scissors cutting all the references to them out of the gospel accounts. But there are less than 20 of what I would call reports of *major* cases of healing. There are no reports of things like ingrown goiters, stiffness of the neck, or desire for alcohol being removed, which are often types of "beneath the surface" healing that is claimed by those who make a profession of it today. Healings such as these may have taken place, but the gospel writers report big-league stuff like withered hands taking their normal shape, blind eyes seeing, deaf ears hearing, speech impediments removed, lepers made whole, a cut-off ear being reattached. There can be no doubt that the healing miracles brought release from physical ailments and handicaps. Besides these major instances, there are many verses that wrap up hosts of unrecorded miracles of healing. "Jesus healed many who had various diseases" (Mark 1:34). "Great crowds came to him, bringing the lame, the blind, the crippled, the mute and many others, and laid them at his feet; and he healed them. The people were amazed when they saw the mute speaking, the crippled made well, the lame walking and the blind seeing. And they praised the God of Israel" (Matt. 15:30–31). John sums it all up this way: "Jesus did many other things as well. If every one of them were written down, I suppose that even the whole world would not have room for the books that would be written" (John 21:25).

Having said that these healing miracles of Jesus were certainly valid instances of release from physical ills, something else must be said so that our understanding of them will not be perverted. For one thing, Jesus did not heal everyone or everything while He was on earth. Because of His poor reception in His home town, for example, Mark says: "He could not do any miracles there, except lay his hands on a few sick people and heal them" (Mark 6:5). Luke says that Jesus likened His action there to that of Elijah, who helped only one widow, though there were many widows in the land, and to that of Elisha, who cleansed only Naaman from leprosy, even though there were many other lepers around (Luke 4:25–27). Luke says that when Jesus cleansed a leper, He told him to keep it quiet. "Yet the news about him spread all the more, so that crowds of people came to hear him and to be healed of their sicknesses. But Jesus often withdrew to lonely places and prayed" (Luke 5:15–16).

The second thing to remember is that those who were healed by Jesus ultimately fell victim to disease at another time and died. Even their miraculous healing was not permanent in this world. Miracles of healing are possible, and God be praised when they occur. But let me underscore this, that continued pain or illness *does by no means* indicate that God has abandoned you. To anyone who turns to God, release will come, or strength and patience to bear the burden.

Fulfillment of Prophecy

The miracle healings were also the fulfillment of prophecy. When Matthew records events of the day when Jesus healed Peter's mother-in-law of a fever and healed and cleansed others, he says, "This was to fulfill what was spoken through the prophet Isaiah: 'He took up our infirmities and carried our diseases' " (Matt. 8:17). It was a prelude to that complete fulfillment of forgiveness and restoration on the cross, when for the whole world Jesus "took up our infirmities and carried our sorrows . . . was pierced for our transgressions . . . crushed for our iniquities" (Is. 53). To assure John the Baptist that He was the promised Messiah, Jesus said to tell John: "The blind receive sight, the lame walk, those who have leprosy are cured, the deaf hear, the dead are raised up, and the good news is preached to the poor" (Matt. 11:5). These "acts" of forgiveness were proof to John that Jesus was the Savior. All these traces and results of sin in the world were erased to dramatize and publicize forgiveness and salvation in Christ.

Dynamic Forgiveness

I call the healing miracles of Jesus "dynamic forgiveness." The phrase "mighty works" comes from the Greek word *dynameis*, which is the root of words in English like *dynamite* and *dynamic*. Jesus said in Luke 10:13: "Woe to you, Korazin! Woe to you, Bethsaida! For if the miracles [*dynameis*] that were performed in you had been performed in Tyre and Sidon, they would have repented long ago, sitting in sackcloth and ashes." Korazin and Bethsaida were cities on the Sea of Galilee where Jesus had performed miracles. His purpose was to bring the people to repentance and forgiveness. The miracles of healing were acts of forgiveness toward the persons healed, but were also lessons in forgiveness for those who witnessed them. But Jesus said there would have been a better response had He done them in pagan cities like Tyre and Sidon. To say that these miracles were dynamic forgiveness, or forgiveness in action, means that through them forgiveness was meant to invade the lives of the healed and of the witnesses.

There are four things about this dynamic forgiveness. First, in some healing miracles, this forgiveness was actually pronounced. We have already looked at the healing of the paralytic (Mark 2:1–2), where Jesus said: "Your sins are forgiven" and then enforced this pronouncement with the man's healing. When He healed the woman who had been bent over for 18 years, Jesus referred to her as "a daughter of Abraham, whom Satan has kept bound for eighteen long years" and said that it was time that she be loosed from this bond (Luke 13:16). When He healed her and said, "Woman, you are set free from your infirmity" (Luke 13:12), it was a pronouncement of forgiveness upon her.

Once when Jesus forgave a prostitute, He said, "Your sins are forgiven. . . . Your faith has saved you; go in peace" (Luke

7:48–49). He used these same words of restoration toward some whom He healed. Blind Bartimaeus made a plea of repentance, "Have mercy on me!" Jesus said to him, "Go, your faith has healed you" (Mark 10:52). Then Bartimaeus received his sight. It was a pronouncement of forgiveness. A woman with a flow of blood for 12 years came up behind and touched His robe and was healed. "The woman, knowing what had happened to her, came and fell at his feet and, trembling with fear, told him the whole truth. He said to her, 'Daughter, your faith has healed you. Go in peace and be freed from your suffering' " (Mark 5:33–34). It was a pronouncement of forgiveness. So it was also with the one grateful leper who was made clean and sent on his way (Luke 17:11–19).

Second, where forgiveness is not pronounced along with healing, it is implied. When Jesus healed the first leper, the leper had said, "If you are willing, you can make me clean." Jesus said, "I am willing. Be clean" (Mark 1:40–41). Then Jesus sent him to the priests to go through the ceremony of cleansing, a ritual that ended with a sin offering of lamb's blood.

A Roman centurion came to Jesus, asking Him to heal a paralyzed servant. He made a profession of unworthiness. He was a Gentile and a soldier. But Jesus said he had more faith than He had seen in Israel and went on to indicate that this man would sit with Abraham in the kingdom of heaven while many "subjects of the kingdom" would be thrown out (Matt. 8:12). "Then Jesus said to the centurion, 'Go! It will be done just as you believed it would.' And his servant was healed at that very hour" (Matt. 8:13). It was more than just a matter of healing the servant. It was an implied acceptance of the centurion by Jesus, a forgiving of the barriers which the centurion thought might exist.

One man whom Jesus healed had lain ill for 38 years (John 5:2–15). Later the same day Jesus saw the man in the temple and said to him, "See, you are well again. Stop sinning or something worse may happen to you." Jesus knew that this man's particular illness was connected with his past life. His healing was evidence that the sins of his past had been forgiven.

On the basis of the miracles where forgiveness is clearly pronounced, and others where forgiveness is strongly implied, it can be said that all the miracles of healing relate to dynamic forgiveness, the mighty work of forgiveness, forgiveness in action. Among the many consequences of sin in the world is the presence of physical disease and infirmity. The healing miracles, which removed these, were a mighty portrayal of the power of Christ to forgive.

One more way to look at this dynamic forgiveness is to see it as a compelling factor with God. God has a compulsion to forgive. It was this compulsion that caused Him to send His only Son into the world to redeem it. God desires to forgive rather than to destroy. One man was born blind (John 9). People said it was either because of his own sin or the sin of his parents. Jesus said it was neither. The purpose of his blindness was not to show God's angry judgment, but rather His mercy. Jesus came not to turn lights off in the world (men would do that with their own rebellion) but to be the Light of the world. To all who thought the blindness was a result of sins, the miracle of seeing would have to mean forgiveness. Yet it wrote a bigger lesson than the forgiveness of only one man. It spelled out God's overwhelming compulsion and willingness to forgive. The lepers being cleansed, the deaf hearing, the impeded voices speaking clearly, and the ruler's son being brought back from the brink of death, withered hands re-forming—all these and more testified that forgiveness is a compelling factor with God.

Fourth, it is a propelling factor with people. Forgiveness is a dynamic, moving force among people. Forgiveness is not an end in itself. It is a retro-rocket that stops men from plummeting away from God and then propels them closer to Him. It also propels a person into closer, more vital relationships and encounters with other people. Christ's words "Go in peace" were not a signal for the forgiven sinner to get lost once again in all the entanglements of his past life. It was and is a powerful send-off to a higher orbit, up and away from the downward pulls of yesterday. The lame man leaping, the one who was blind now striding along in new confidence, the one who was a leper now no longer apologizing for being alive, the woman who was bent over now walking straight and tall before men and God—all these were more than just physical changes. Forgiveness had touched their lives and given them newness on the inside to match the newness on the outside. Forgiveness is not a stagnant proclamation. It is a dynamic propellant surpassing anything else in the ability to get people going.

Foretaste of Heaven

We have said that the miracles of healing were physical release, a fulfillment of prophecy, and a dynamic forgiveness. Finally, they were a foretaste of heaven. Each healing was, in a sense, a return to Paradise, temporary for sure, for the ones healed were not removed from a sinful world. But the healings were a preview of that complete restoration pictured in Rev. 21:1–4:

> "Then I saw a new heaven and a new earth, for the first heaven and the first earth had passed away, and there was no longer any sea. I saw the Holy City, the new Jerusalem, coming down out of heaven from God, prepared as a bride beautifully dressed for her husband. And I heard a loud voice from the throne saying, "Now the dwelling of God is with men, and he will live with them. They will be his people, and God himself will be with them and be their God. He will wipe away every tear from their eyes. There will be no more death or mourning or crying or pain, for the old order of things has passed away."

Any healing that comes in this life is a foretaste of heaven. Healing that does not come will make heaven seem all the more grand.

A Word About "Divine" Healing

Several years ago I heard an Air Force chaplain speak on the subject of divine healing. I still remember his closing statement: "I believe in divine healing because all healing is divine." God is terribly shortchanged when it comes to being properly credited for healing. I suppose that 95 percent of the prayers for healing uttered at the bedside of patients are answered with the patient being released and returning home well or much improved. Yet this is often labeled "natural" recovery, while a case of "divine" healing must be attested to by a patient leaping from his bed and running from the hospital with sheets and blankets adragging.

How can such unfairness to God be avoided? Here is one way. Whenever you have an ailment, large or small, take your case to Jesus first of all. A simple prayer will do: "Lord Jesus, I want You to be my Specialist. You are the Great Physician, and I am glad You will take my case. Thank You for the relief I'll experience, no matter how or how soon it will come." The ailment may ease without medication. The help may come after a visit to the doctor or a trip to the hospital. In any event, you will relate the relief to your original "Specialist's" care for you, and your healing will be properly credited.

As a further step of placing yourself under His care in special need, you may wish to request anointing with oil and prayer for healing. The words of James 5:14–15 sound like it was routine practice at that time, and not at all a strange or far-out ritual. I like to look at it this way—if you knew a friend was coming to your house, but you weren't sure just when he might arrive, you would want him to feel welcome. You might put up signs at all the entrance doors. You wouldn't want any entrance to seem blocked to him. To be anointed with oil simply says, "Lord, I want to be open to any way You may choose to help me." Healing may come at that moment. If it does not, the person can still have the relaxed assurance of having put up the welcome sign on any entrance the Lord may use in bringing help and healing. It has been my experience that anointing is a holy moment in itself as the person is marked again with the sign placed on him at baptism. There is a grand return to the ground of God's love and forgiveness, and this solid ground is needed when the earth beneath you shakes with serious hurt or trouble. It has also been my experience that good always follows such anointing, sometimes in amazing physical help. I have never known a person to regret the experience.

A Word About "Faith" Healing

Faith can be a problem in faith healing. It can be a problem if faith centers in the sick person. I have followed a trail of troubled people who were zealously mistreated and misinformed. They were told that Jesus was never sick because He had perfect faith and was without sin. Therefore sickness is proof that either a person has inadequate faith or unconfessed sin. When healing does not take place, these poor victims of spiritual quacks are left with their maladies plus agony of spirit. The "faith-healer's" record remains intact, because any lack of healing is not his fault, but the fault of his faithless, sinful patients.

Faith is also a problem if it centers on the problem. There is a lesson to learn from Bartimaeus when he said, "Son of David, have mercy on me" (Mark 10:48). He did not say, "I'm blind, and I am exercising great personal faith in asking you to make these blind eyes see." A similar lesson may be learned from the leper who said, "Lord, if you are willing, you can make me clean" (Matt.

8:2). He did not say, "I am convinced that all my leprous sores will disappear, so go ahead and prove me to be right." "Faith" in faith healing is bigger than a faith directed to a lump or pain. It is faith directed to a Lord who is compassionate and powerful. If the pain subsides, it is the Lord, not my faith, who must be acknowledged. If the pain persists, it is not a judgment upon my faith. I must then only lean harder upon my Lord, in whom I believe with the full assurance that He has not deserted me.

A friend has cancer. There have been several "prophecies" that he will be healed. He has been told to accept and thank God for his healing even though the signs and symptoms remain and increase (no New Testament healing involved such sanctimonious pretending). My friend feels he is letting down the Christian community that has been praying for him. What is the matter? Isn't he "believing" enough? I admit to him that neither one of us knows the end of the story. Healing may come, and we will celebrate together. But healing may not come. Then we will sorrow together, but not without hope. In the meantime, I tell my friend, there are dozens of people who are grateful for the witness he is giving as a man of faith in the midst of great trial and pain. A tear forms in his eye, and he thanks me.

No miracle here? Of course there is a miracle. Regardless of the matter of healing, there is the great miracle of a mortal man now assured of an eternal destiny because he is a forgiven, restored child of the heavenly Father. The answer to why some are healed and others are not resides in the mind of a sovereign God. But that same sovereign God has openly willed that the greater miracle of eternal health and welfare be the experience of every person.

Something to think/talk/pray about

—Miracles of healing are possible, but continued illness or pain does not indicate that God has abandoned you. Is this statement true and helpful, or is it a cop-out?

—God has a compulsion to forgive. How does that make you feel?

—How is forgiveness not an end, but a beginning?

—Healing that comes through the Specialist (Jesus) or through specialists (doctors) is equally divine.

6. Prelude in F Major (Miracles of Raising the Dead)

Our task so far has been to see the miracles of Jesus as forgiveness. Now we shall look at His miracles of raising the dead. Our theme is "Prelude in F Major." For our purposes F Major is forgiveness, for it is the major key in which all the miracles of Jesus are played. According to definition, a prelude is "something done to prepare the way for something important." This also describes the miracles of raising the dead. Having said that, however, it must be admitted that they were also significant in themselves. The three specific cases of raising the dead mentioned in the gospels describe situations of close family relationships. Jairus' daughter was only 12. She was dying before Jairus came to Jesus, and had died before they returned to Jairus' house. People met them on the way with the harsh report, "Your daughter is dead. Why bother the teacher any more?" (Mark 5:35). People at the house were "crying and wailing loudly." Only Peter, John, James, and the father and mother went with Jesus into the room where the dead child lay. "Talitha koum!" This means, "Little girl, I say to you, get up!" And as the girl rose up and walked around, so rose all the hopes and dreams of a mother and father that had so recently been crushed into the ground.

Luke reports the raising of the widow's son at Nain. She was terribly alone in the world and walked dejectedly along the way to bury her only son. To the mother Jesus said, "Don't cry." And to the son, "Young man, I say to you, get up!" The dead man sat up and began to speak. And He gave him to his mother (Luke 7:11–17). Who would belittle the significance of this reunion?

The third instance of raising the dead involved Lazarus (John 11:1–44). He was an only brother on whom two sisters, Mary and

Martha, were dependent. Lazarus was also a very close personal friend of Jesus. Unless you discount what friendship with another human being meant to Jesus, it must be admitted that Lazarus' restoration to life was a joy both to the sisters and to Jesus Himself. In fact, John later records Jesus and Lazarus enjoying a dinner together in Bethany (John 12:1–2).

As meaningful as these cases were in very human, touching situations, there was something that transcended their strictly earthly significance. They were preludes, things done to prepare the way for something greater.

Death's reign had continued for a long time. When God first created man, there was but one restriction—not to eat of the tree of the knowledge of good and evil. The consequence of disobedience would be death: "When you eat of it you will surely die" (Gen. 2:17). When the fall of man occurred, another tree had to be placed out of bounds, lest men live forever as fallen, sinful creatures. This was the tree of life. This sad precaution is described by the writer of Genesis this way: "The Lord God said, 'The man has now become like one of us, knowing good and evil. He must not be allowed to reach out his hand and take also from the tree of life and eat, and live forever.' So the Lord God banished him from the Garden of Eden, to work the ground from which he had been taken. After he drove the man out, he placed on the east side of the Garden of Eden cherubim and a flaming sword flashing back and forth to guard the way to the tree of life" (Gen. 3:22–24). The stage of the world on which life alone was meant to play was now reset, and the atmosphere of death hung over every act of man. Paul put it this way: "Just as sin entered the world through one man, and death through sin, and in this way death came to all men, because all sinned . . . by the trespass of the one man, death reigned through that one man . . ." (Rom. 5:12, 17).

The reign continued unbroken, unchallenged until Jesus came. Satan said, "The kingdom of this world is mine, and death is the sign of my rule." Jesus came saying, "The kingdom of this world will become the kingdom of My God, and life shall be the sign of victory!" The miracles of raising the dead were preludes to this ultimate victory. Just as the Normandy beachhead planted seeds of victory for the Allies and seeds of defeat for the enemy, so these miracles proclaimed a new master over death.

There was an artist in Kalispell, Montana, who painted little pictures on canvas boards about 6 by 8 inches. He also painted pictures that were nearly as large as an average living room wall. The little ones carried hints of the larger scenes. The miracles of raising the dead did the same thing. They were impressive pictures, but only small ones that hinted of a greater scene to be revealed later.

They were a prelude to Christ's own resurrection. Lazarus' rising was the rising of one. Jairus' daughter was a single resurrection. The widow's son rose up from the dead, but no other dead accompanied him. But with Christ's rising, there would be the hope for all men to share in this victory. "As in Adam all die, so in Christ all will be made alive" (1 Cor. 15:22).

The miracles of raising the dead were also a prelude to the general resurrection. In the miracles we have cited, the picture is drawn with a few strokes involving three people. In the general resurrection, however, all will be involved in a resurrection of judgment or glory. "A time is coming," Jesus said, "when all who are in their graves will hear his [the Son of God's] voice and come out—those who have done good will rise to live, and those who have done evil will rise to be condemned" (John 5:28–29). Not only will it be a general resurrection, but unlike those raised while Jesus was on earth, those in the final resurrection will not die again. "They can no longer die," Jesus said, "for they are like the angels. They are God's children, since they are children of the resurrection" (Luke 20:36). The passage in Revelation that speaks of the new earth without tears or pain includes the promise: "There will be no more death" (Rev. 21:4). This final proclamation of joy replaces that sad precaution where the angel had to guard the tree of life against man. The miracles of raising the dead hinted at the return to God's original intent that life, not death, should reign.

Yet these miracles were only hints, only preludes of something greater to come. And they were temporary. Jairus' daughter, the widow's son, and Lazarus all died again. They now await with all the dead the final "great getting-up morning." In fact, Lazarus walked with his life in peril from the time he came out of the tomb. There were many witnesses when he was raised from the dead; so many, in fact, that word was spreading to the point that the Pharisees said the whole world was going after Jesus (John 12:17–19). The chief priests decided that their only hope of stopping this rush was to remove the attraction. So, ironically, they plotted to put Lazarus to death— again! (John 12:10). It is not indicated whether they were ever successful, but, in time, Lazarus did go the way of all flesh.

When you begin studying these miracles, it is rather impressive how few indications there are of the dead being raised. There are some general references to this taking place.("Jesus replied, 'Go back and report to John what you hear and see: The blind receive sight, the lame walk, those who have leprosy are cured, the deaf hear, the dead are raised, and the good news is preached to the poor' " [Matt. 11:4–5].) There is indication that the 12 disciples were given this power. ("These twelve Jesus sent out with the following instructions: . . . 'Heal the sick, raise the dead, cleanse those who have leprosy, drive out demons' " [Matt. 10:5, 8].) Dead saints came out of their tombs at Jesus' death and resurrection. ("At that moment the curtain of the temple was torn in two from top to bottom. The earth shook and the rocks split. The tombs broke open and the bodies of many holy people who had died were raised to life. They came out of the tombs, and after Jesus' resurrection they went into the holy city and appeared to many people." [Matt. 27:51–53].) But you would think that this astounding power would be displayed at every occasion to enhance and impress the message of redemption. This is not the case, however. There are some instances where a miracle of raising the dead would have seemed especially fitting. Surely if the martyred John the Baptist had been restored to life, it would have made an impact on the people. Jesus paid tribute to John, but John was not raised. And if only the one thief on the cross next to Jesus could have been released from the cross, strong and alive, to witness to his new faith in the Lord! But the thief was told that the promises would be fulfilled on the other side of death. Paradise would not be found this side of physical death.

Jesus once told a story about a rich man and a poor man named Lazarus, not the one raised from the dead, however. They both died. Lazarus was comforted in the bosom of Abraham, and the rich man was in torment in Hades. The rich man wanted to warn his brothers not to make the same mistakes he had made in his selfish life. He got the idea that Lazarus should go back and tell them. Luke records the story (16:19–31). "[The rich man said:] 'Then I beg you, father, send Lazarus to my father's house, for I have five brothers. Let him warn them, so that they will not also come to this place of torment.' Abraham replied, 'They have Moses and the Prophets; let them listen to them.' 'No, father Abraham,' he said, 'but if someone from the dead goes to them, they will repent.' He said to him, 'If they do not listen to Moses and the Prophets, they will not be convinced even if someone rises from the dead' " (Luke 16:27–31).

I have never seen anyone raised from the dead. But I have seen the hardness of people's hearts. I have seen people experience the return of a loved one from the brink of death, and yet make no lasting grateful response to God. I have seen the death of a family member cause only fleeting repentance or turning to God. God has made known His love and mercy in so many ways. No person needs any more convincing steps taken by God. Each person needs only to take the steps of repentance and faith toward Him. If you have set your heart against Him, don't wait for a miracle to convince you. You would get around that, too, and keep from surrendering.

While studying these miracles, I received two impressions I want to share with you. One is disturbing and the other is comforting.

You and I don't need such miracles to be part of our lives. I don't have to have power to raise the dead. I don't have to be a Lazarus and experience being raised from the dead. Because right now, without either of these, I have the greatest gift God could give me—the gift of life is mine now. It is yours, too. The big question is, What are you doing with it? What am I doing with it? Are we doing enough with these lives God has given us so that it would be worth God's while to raise us from the dead so that our lives might continue? That question can be disturbing.

But there is another thought that has been with me. When I read about my Lord shouting into the tomb, "Lazarus, come out!" or saying to the widow's son, "Young man, I say to you, get up!" or taking the hand of the child and saying, "Little girl, I say to you, get up!" it is a comfort and a thrill to know He will say that to me one day, and to you. When He does, He has no desire to have to say, "Arise, and be judged for your faithlessness and ungodliness!" He wants to say: "Come, you who are blessed by my Father; take your inheritance, the kingdom prepared for you since the creation of the world" (Matt. 25:34).

Jesus' miracles of raising the dead composed a beautiful prelude of forgiveness that moved toward a symphony of salvation written on the cross and empty tomb.

We have been missing two opportunities to witness to this strong hope. The scene for both is the cemetery. One opportunity is in the Christian committal service. It is an ideal time to confess the Creed "on location" and in the face of evidence to the contrary. "I believe . . . in the forgiveness of sins, the resurrection of the body, and the life everlasting. Amen."

The second opportunity is afforded by the gravestone. Most have only two dates carved on them—birth and death. For the Christian, the most important date has been omitted—the date of baptism. It is a beginning date that requires no ending date to follow. In silent, solid stone, it would witness to the great Easter that awaits all who have died in the Lord.

Something to think/talk/pray about

—Why can a Christian funeral be called a "celebration"?
—Walk through a cemetery and note any resurrection hope that is evident in symbols or words on gravestones.
—What do you think about having a baptismal date on the tombstone?

7. Forgiveness: Storming the Fortress (Miracles of Casting Out Demons)

In the several studies we have made so far on miracles, we have never had to begin by considering whether a problem really existed. In studying the nature miracles, we never questioned whether storms or hunger are part of the real world. In the healing miracles there was no doubt that people suffered pain or endured handicaps. In the miracles of raising the dead, the fact of death never had to be established.

Now we turn to Jesus' miracles of casting out demons. Having said that, we *do* have to begin by questioning the reality of demons. This is prompted by our own apprehensions, our own lack of evidence and experience. However, if the Bible is any basis for our accepting the fact of storms, sickness, death, that is, if we take as valid reporting the accounts in Scripture of Jesus' encounter with these earthly realities, then we must on the same basis assume the validity of demons, whether explainable or not. To dismiss the validity of these accounts of unclean spirits would be to place every other type of miracle under the same suspicion. Demons are mentioned as matter-of-factly as other human maladies. Demons are given the same credence as are angels. The devil is as much a reality as God. If Scripture is revealed truth, then revelation regarding the power of evil carries the same weight of authority as does revelation regarding God's love.

In a *New York Times* article entitled "God Is Alive and Well in America" (12-29-68), the results of a Gallup Poll survey were discussed. "Ninety-eight percent of the Americans surveyed, for instance, said that they believe in God; 73 percent believe in life after death; 65 percent believe in hell; 60 percent believe in the Devil." (British statistics: 77 percent believe in God, 38 percent believe in life after death, 23 percent believe in hell, and 21 percent believe in the devil.) The poll failed to give the basis for believing, however. I am afraid that the basis was simply personal reactions to these doctrines. The basis obviously was *not* the Bible, for the Bible does not give the option of 98 percent belief in God over against a 60 percent belief in the devil. The Bible insists upon the 100 percent reality of God and Satan and their respective forces and agents.

If the problems presented in the various miracles must be equally valid, so must the solutions. If the storms were quieted, the hungry fed, the sick healed, the dead raised, then the demons were cast out. We may choose to dismiss the demon bit, but we cannot give good reason for such a sophisticated exclusion.

I would suggest the same approach when updating these things that we read about in Scripture. Storms are still current, sickness is not out of style, death is still in vogue. And we have no reason to insist that the demonic has become passé. It would surely be naive to say that the advancements of the 20th century have outpaced evil and left demonic forces lost in the dust. God is not dead. Neither is Satan. God's Holy Spirit is operative in the world—so is the spirit of evil. Neither angels nor demons have gone into retirement. I am not encouraging anyone at this point to become an expert in recognizing people with demons. I am saying that we can all stand to be more alert to manifestations of both good *and* evil powers in the world around us.

You get no farther along in Scripture than the first two chapters of Genesis before encountering the first case of demon possession. God's man and woman were soon prey to the devil—fallen prey. Eve explained her disobedience this way, "The serpent deceived me, and I ate" (Gen. 3:13). One created to be God-possessed had become devil-possessed. Yet even before the Fall, God had set in motion His plan of salvation. He would repossess His own, and forgiveness would initiate this repossession.

Matt. 12:22–32 records Jesus' explanation of how the casting out of demons was a proclamation of forgiveness. A certain man had three strikes against him—he was blind, he couldn't speak, and he evidenced demon possession. When Jesus cast out the demon, the other physical difficulties were also removed. The Pharisees immediately made a charge that was rather absurd. They accused Jesus of being in partnership with the prince of demons and gave this as the reason for His being able to cast them out. But this accusation did not make sense. If, for instance, the police in a city made a raid on a gambling operation, it would be illogical to conclude that the police were on the side of gambling. This would be the case if the raid did *not* take place. But raiding the operation would show that the police opposed it and did not condone it. Likewise, when Jesus cast out demons, He acted as an enemy of Satan, not a cohort. "If I drive out demons by the Spirit of God," Jesus said, "then the kingdom of God has come upon you" (Matt. 12:28).

The casting out of demons was a sign that Satan's power was now challenged and opposed. In very graphic words Jesus continued, "How can anyone enter a strong man's house and carry off his possessions unless he first ties up the strong man? Then he can rob his house" (Matt. 12:29). The strong man was Satan, his house was the power of evil, the goods were fallen man, and the plunderer was Jesus, with His weapon, the Holy Spirit. He stormed the fortress of the devil and released forgiveness as the new air for former prisoners to breathe. It is in this same connection that Jesus mentions sinning against the Holy Spirit. Whoever blasphemes the Spirit is turning off the very source of power necessary to overcome Satan and his evil forces.

The demons themselves recognized the lordship of Jesus and His authority. "Have you come to destroy us?" they asked (Luke 4:34). The very question showed that they already knew the answer. Yes, He had come to destroy them and overcome evil. Luke says (4:41): "Demons also came out of many people, shouting, 'You are the Son of God!' But he rebuked them and would not allow them to speak, because they knew he was the Christ." When Luke tells of a demon-possessed man among the Gerasenes being cleansed, he says that the demons begged Jesus "not to order them to go into the Abyss" (Luke 8:31). They knew He had this authority. Jesus allowed them to enter a herd of swine, but it was a temporary home. The swine rushed into the sea, drowned, and we can assume that the evil spirits were then committed to their own kind of prison.

Both the awful absence of forgiveness and the awesome

power of forgiveness are impressively displayed in this case. The people showed the absence of forgiveness—toward Jesus for causing the swine's death and toward the man for his past life. They showed no happiness over his restoration, and they asked Jesus to leave their neighborhood. It was the man who demonstrated the power of forgiveness. While his countrymen begged Jesus to leave, he begged Jesus for permission to go along with Him. But Jesus saw that his greatest service would be in proclaiming his personal experience of cleansing and forgiveness: " 'Go home to your family and tell them how much the Lord has done for you, and how he has had mercy on you.' So the man went away and began to tell in the Decapolis how much Jesus had done for him. And all the people were amazed" (Mark 5:19–20). Like the woman who came and washed Jesus' feet with her tears and wiped them with her hair, this man loved much because he had been forgiven much.

Similar to his case was Mary Magdalene. She must have had a severe case of demon possession. Her name is hardly ever mentioned without the accompanying statement that seven demons had been cast out of her. She served Jesus while He was on preaching missions (Luke 8:2) and was among the first to seek to anoint His body early Easter Sunday. She loved much because she had been forgiven much.

Especially in the case of the Gerasene man and Mary Magdalene, the casting out of demons acted out what the assurance of pardon should do and mean to everyone. They were new creatures. The evil spirits were replaced by a forgiving spirit and a forgiven spirit. I can imagine that both the man and Mary Magdalene did not always have an easy time of it after their cleansing. People have ways of reacting to a person as he used to be, in spite of what he may be now. Their attitude does not update to the present situation. I once heard a man tell about "after-care" work he does with young people who have been released from corrective institutions. Usually these young people are placed in other than their home towns because people's former attitudes toward these kids would hang on and keep them from having the fresh start they need so badly. I rather think both the man and Mary knew such pressure. "There goes that crazy guy. He used to run naked in the cemetery!" "There's crazy Mary. Hi, crazy Mary!" Yet these people, concentrating on those who had been demon-possessed, failed to see their own cases of demon possession, for to have an unforgiving spirit is to have an evil spirit. An unforgiving spirit is an evil spirit. So is an unforgiven spirit. The person who knows nothing of forgiveness, or the person who hears forgiveness proclaimed so much but is immune and unaffected by it—who possesses such a one? God doesn't!

It is the power of evil that hardens a person so that he has no grateful response to forgiveness—and this deadening, evil spirit operates aggressively right within the church where the message of forgiveness is proclaimed. Take any congregation as an example. Compare its *potential* as an instrument of God with its *accomplishments*. There is no other explanation but that demonic forces are holding back the people of God from being what they are called to be. You don't have to start with a weird case of demon possession. Start with an average member of the church. Let him go through a lifetime with only minimum response to God, with only halfhearted discipleship, with little commitment and little desire to be used by God, and you have a person who has been more under influences of evil spirits than of angels. On the other hand, start again with an average church member, give him a desire to be God's person whatever the changes or costs involved, and you will have something just as dramatic as any of the miracles of demon cleansing.

In the early Genesis account the Fall is the result of man coming under the authority of Satan. But when Jesus came, He not only exerted authority over Satan's representatives, but He gave His disciples this same awesome authority. "The seventy-two returned with joy and said, 'Lord, even the demons submit to us in your name' " (Luke 10:17). The demons subject to them—this was a real turnabout, and in it was evidence that a new lordship had begun in the world. That lordship continues. Victims turn into victors! That exciting option is open to everyone in Jesus' name. We have been freed from the powers of evil that our lives might be lived for God and good. The key is to crown *Him* Lord of all!

Exorcism is now a bad word, even in the church. That's unfortunate. What has become the possession of the kooky was originally the birthright of the Christian. At Ephesus there is an excavated baptismal room from the Church of St. Mary. Converts stood in white robes, facing east, at the top of the steps. Three times they said with new resolve, "Devil, I leave you." Then they walked down into the baptistry and went under the water three times at the words, "In the name of the Father and of the Son and of the Holy Spirit." The first action of our Christ-related life was similarly an exorcism: "Do you renounce the devil and all his works and ways? Yes, I renounce them!" Since that time we have both the right and responsibility to continue renouncing and exorcising him.

When something that should be in constant use becomes unused, there arises in its stead misuse and abuse. This is the case with the casting out of demons. I attended a meeting in Kansas City that hosted a "specialist" in casting out demons. It was a wild show that could have been called "Name That Demon." In preparation, ushers actually distributed Kleenex boxes, stacks of paper towels, and hosts of wastebaskets up and down the aisles. The specialist would name categories of demons, and at a given command the audience was to cough, spit, and vomit up the demons. In the course of the evening he named at least 300, and one certain lady didn't miss a single one. She was the coughingest Christian I have ever seen. A gentle, 70-year-old lady, raised in the Pentecostal tradition, sat quietly beside me through the whole service. After the service she said in a beautiful understatement, "I don't believe all of that is quite necessary, do you?" I agreed. Then we talked together of how Jesus is like a Commander-in-Chief of an army. If He so desires, He may give a specific order by name to Privates Smith and Jones and they had better move. On the other hand, He can give one general command and move the entire army—and Smith and Jones had better not try saying, "We don't have to obey you, Commander, because you didn't call our name!"

Our Lord has majestic authority over the enemy. It may be that at some time a demon is helpfully named. That is, if jealousy is a special harassment to me, it may weaken its hold when I confront it and talk of it openly and honestly. But instead of playing "Name That Demon" or giving the enemy too much attention (remember that what gets your attention ultimately gets you), it is much better to celebrate the lordship of Christ and the freedom that is ours in Him.

Something to think/talk/pray about

—Somewhere I heard this chorus:
"Each time I flee to His atoning blood,
He ever lives to make His promise good.

Though all the host of hell march in
To make a second claim,
They'll all march out at the mention of His name."
—The world gives more attention to evil than to good, and the
church gives more attention to demons than to angels. Do you
agree?

8. The Reincarnation of Forgiveness (the Lord's Supper)

When evening came, Jesus was reclining at the table with the Twelve. And while they were eating, he said, "I tell you the truth, one of you will betray me." They were very sad and began to say to him one after the other, "Surely not I, Lord?" Jesus replied, "The one who has dipped his hand into the bowl with me will betray me. The Son of Man will go just as it is written about him. But woe to that man who betrays the Son of Man! It would be better for him if he had not been born." Then Judas, the who would betray him, said, "Surely not I, Rabbi?" Jesus answered, "Yes, it is you." While they were eating, Jesus took bread, gave thanks and broke it, and gave it to his disciples, saying, "Take, and eat; this is my body." Then he took the cup, gave thanks and offered it to them, saying, "Drink from it, all of you. This is my blood of the covenant, which is poured out for many for the forgiveness of sins. I tell you, I will not drink of this fruit of the vine from now on until that day when I drink it anew with you in my Father's kingdom" (Matt. 26:20–29).

It took a stupendous miracle to create the universe, but the miracle of God's love in our redemption is far greater. That's the kind of miracle we are talking about now—a miracle of love and grace, and forgiveness is the atmosphere in which this miracle takes place. We have defined a miracle as "an act or happening in the material or physical sphere that apparently departs from the laws of nature or goes beyond what is known concerning these laws." There are two areas we will consider. In both, Jesus departed from or went beyond what we would term the natural. I refer first to Jesus' attitude. It is a departure from what would be the normal or natural attitude of human beings. When wronged, it is in the very nature of man to want revenge, or to insist on something from the wrongdoer to make up for the wrong. But with Jesus a spirit of forgiveness always overrode the spirit of revenge. His was an "in spite of" forgiveness that came from a heart of love, and not a "because of" forgiveness that waits until the other party has done something to deserve forgiveness. He showed forgiveness in the face of the greatest betrayal and the most outright denial.

The text begins with Jesus' reference to Judas as the betrayer. There is no indication that Jesus would have turned Judas away had he come back seeking forgiveness. We once talked of forgiveness as being dynamic, effective, active. We can see this especially in the case of Judas and Peter. You can't escape being changed by forgiveness. It will have its effect on you—for good or for evil. If you can't accept it, it will harden you. It did this to Judas, and in despair he went out and hanged himself.

Peter, in his denial of Jesus, committed an act very similar to betrayal. It was a refusal to identify himself with One who loved him very much. Jesus' love followed Peter, too, but instead of becoming hardened and despairing, Peter accepted this unnatural love of his Lord and was reformed, transformed by it. In his First Letter, Peter, writing years after this taste of Jesus' forgiving love, still seems overwhelmed by it. He knows a Lord who with perfect justice could have written him off, but who instead reclaimed him. These are Peter's words: " 'He committed no sin, and no deceit was found in his mouth.' When they hurled their insults at him, he did not retaliate; when he suffered, he made no threats. Instead, he entrusted himself to him who judges justly. He himself bore our sins in his body on the tree, so that we might die to sins and live for righteousness; by his wounds you have been healed. For you were like sheep going astray, but now you have returned to the Shepherd and Overseer of your souls" (1 Peter 2:22–25). Peter knew what that return was like; he had walked that road of forgiveness back to his Lord.

Jesus' *attitude* was a miracle of love and grace. So was His *action* as He instituted the Lord's Supper. On the night before

His flesh and blood would be consumed in death, He spoke these words, "Take and eat . . . my body. . . . Drink . . . my blood." This giving of Himself was in the atmosphere of forgiveness— "poured out for many for the forgiveness of sins."

We referred to Jesus' incarnation as forgiveness in the flesh. His coming to earth, being born of a woman, was forgiveness incarnate. Now the institution of the Lord's Supper represented a reincarnation of forgiveness. Reincarnation is usually connected with some oriental belief about people being reborn and on earth again in some other physical form than what they were originally. I do not mean this kind of reincarnation. The word literally means "to invest anew in bodily form." It is in this sense that Holy Communion can be spoken of as the reincarnation of forgiveness. Jesus came once in the flesh. As you take His body and blood, He comes once again—in your flesh. We call the church the body of Christ, and how well this describes the church if Christ is in the believer and the believer in Christ.

But there is another way in which there is a reincarnation of forgiveness as we come to Holy Communion. The Lord walks the earth no more except in and through His people, you and me. His miracle of love and grace is evident in the world through our lives. When Christ dwells in you, the natural feelings of vengeance and retribution are diluted by a new sense of love and a willingness to forgive. To explain this miracle of love and grace in your life is as hard as explaining the miracle of Jesus' giving His body to you in the Sacrament. But it is no less real.

Claim the reality of His promise that He gives you His body and blood and that He seeks to dwell in you so that your life may be a reflection of His.

There are two special meanings that have come to me lately from the words of Jesus: "Do this in remembrance of me." One deals with the reality of recall. I read somewhere that the words may be taken in this sense: "Do this when you want Me here." That makes it so much more than some act of my memory. Instead of bringing back a thought, the Sacrament brings a person back to me. In Holy Communion, Jesus has promised to be on call to His church. "Do this when you want Me here." For the sacramentally oriented Christian this fits meaningfully into the conviction of the real presence of Christ in the bread and wine.

The second meaning also deals with His body, but this time His body, the church. The words could be put this way: "Do this to re-member Me." When the people of God gather for Holy Communion, the body of Christ is re-membered. It is in itself an experience of being His body, but also it is an etching deeper into everyone's awareness just what the church is.

I was once part of a group of chaplains of various denominations. Most of us desired a closing worship together. Because we had become close in other ways, many longed for an experience of the Eucharist. It did not happen. One chaplain (a Catholic priest) expressed his dismay by saying: "Why don't we gather for a service of the Word? Then when it is time for Holy Communion, we'll set up 28 separate tables, each do our own thing, and then come back together to pray that the day will come when we don't have to so divide the body!"

There must be that continued longing in the heart of Jesus as His fragmented body repeats the words that contain the very clue to wholeness—"Do this to re-member Me." His prayer to the Father was for a grand eventual reincarnation in the best sense—"that all of them may be one, Father, just as you are in me and I am in you. May they also be in us so that the world may believe that you have sent me" (John 17:21).

Something to think/talk/pray about

—Forgiveness reforms or deforms, depending on whether it is accepted or rejected.

—Does the word *reincarnation* seem appropriate in relation to the sacrament of Holy Communion?

—Should the Lord's Supper be a goal of Christian unity, or a means of bringing it about? How about looking at it as an *expression* of unity?

9. Jesus' Death— A Miracle of Forgiveness (the Crucifixion)

Death a miracle? How can death be a miracle? Death is the absence of miracles. Death takes place when the hoped-for miracle doesn't happen. "Only a miracle could save him now," says the distressed wife at her husband's deathbed. But there is no miracle. The man dies, and no one considers that a miracle. And, of course, in every instance but one, death is not a miracle. A miracle is something that occurs against or above the usual laws of nature. Death is in no way an exception to the rule. It *is* the rule. "Man is destined to die once" (Heb. 9:27). "Just as sin entered the world through one man, and death through sin . . . in this way death came to all men, because all sinned" (Rom. 5:12).

All the miracles we have looked at so far have been opposing death. The miracle of calming the wind and sea saved the disciples from perishing in the storm. The miracle of feeding the multitude in the wilderness was performed to keep them from falling in exhaustion on their way home. The miracles of healing spared the sick from being victims of their diseases. The miracles of cleansing from demons pulled those possessed off the course that was leading them to sure destruction. The miracles of raising the dead retrieved people from the very clutches of death.

Why then suddenly refer to death as a miracle? Because there was one single death that surely was a miracle. The death of Jesus went against every law that applied to Him. He was truly man. Every other man was created from the dust and was bound for the dust once more. No man was marked as an exception; that is, no one but the man Jesus. He came to earth born of a woman, yet without the stain of sin that labeled every other person born into this world. As He lived and walked on earth, He did not become infected with sin, whose certain wages is death, always paid in full. He knew no sin, and remained in perfect relationship with His heavenly Father. Man had sinned, and the way to the tree of life was barred, so that he would not go on forever as a fallen creature. But Jesus had no sentence of death upon Him because of disobedience. There was no reason that He should ever die. Should He die, it would be as much a miracle as if a sinful man should not die. That death should claim this Sinless One as a victim was surely a miracle.

It was a miracle from another standpoint. Jesus was not only the Possessor of the gift of life, He was the very Source of it. He called Himself this. "I am . . . the life" (John 14:6). John said, "In him was life, and that life was the light of men" (John 1:4). Paul described Jesus in these lofty words: "By him all things were created: things in heaven and on earth, visible and invisible, whether thrones or powers or rulers or authorities; all things were created by him and for him. He is before all things, and in him all things hold together" (Col. 1:16–17). He had claimed existence before father Abraham by saying, "Before Abraham was born, I am" (John 8:58). How could this be true and He still die? Those who mocked Jesus while He was on the cross remembered some of the claims that He had made, and they said in derision, "Let this Christ, this King of Israel, come down now from the cross, that we may see and believe" (Mark 15:32). With thoughts of scorn they must have talked of what a miracle this was, that the King of Israel, who should live forever, was now dying on the cross, with nothing stopping it! And if those who hated Him and never believed thought this way, think how torn the believers must have been at this point. They had accepted His words. He had become life to them. Now His dying was a sort of terrible miracle, something they had not expected would ever happen. In their hearts were the same, but sincere, words that the mockers spoke: "Lord Jesus Christ, our King, come down from the cross. Do not die." But the miracle happened. The Lord of life died.

"God Is Dead." Do you remember seeing that black cover of a *Time* magazine carrying these words in bold print? There were all kinds of reactions. Some undoubtedly agreed. Others laughed it off as some kind of joke. Others became alarmed and annoyed at such a sacrilegious statement. I could never understand, much less agree with, the so-called "God is dead" theologians, but I am one on Good Friday. Such a cover would make a fitting bulletin for a Good Friday service. It sounds preposterous. It sounds impossible. Any miracle does. The death of Jesus was a miracle because it was God the Son dying for the world.

This leads us to a second consideration. Jesus' death—forgiveness? How can death be forgiveness? When a criminal is sentenced to die for a crime, his only hope is a stay of execution. If this is granted, then he has, in a way, been forgiven of his crime. At least the penalty of paying for it with his life is removed. But in no way would it seem to be forgiveness if there was no intervention and the execution was carried out. Death is ordinarily the inevitable consequence of sin.

But let us return to that scene where the convicted criminal awaits the guards who will come and escort him to the death chamber. When the guards come, they bring with them another man. This man takes his place in the cell, and the convicted man is escorted out, not to the execution chamber but to the prison gate. He is released, told that he can go free. The other man has agreed to die in his place for the crime committed. Now death *has* become forgiveness for the one who should have died for his crime. So the death of Jesus is forgiveness for all men. Any person who desires may pay the penalties for his own sin. He need not leave his cell or escape the sentence. He may collect the wages of his sin, and the wages is death. But a death has already taken place. This death has been accepted as full payment for transgressions, and the sinner may walk the corridor of forgiveness to gates of freedom he has never known before.

Jesus once spoke about how His death would be forgiveness and salvation: "I am the good shepherd. The good shepherd lays down his life for the sheep. . . . The reason my Father loves me is that I lay down my life—only to take it up again. No one takes it from me, but I lay it down of my own accord. I have authority to lay it down and authority to take it up again" (John 10:11, 17–18).

All the miracles we have studied so far have been those that Jesus performed. The truth is that He also performed the miracle of His own death. No one else performed this miracle of killing God, of snuffing out Him who was Life itself, of forcing Him to suffer the penalty He did not deserve. No one took His life from Him. He gave it away—that accounts for the miracle. He gave it away to pay for the sins of the world—that accounts for the forgiveness. On Good Friday we commemorate that miracle. We stand confronted by its mystery, feel the power of God's love in this act of Christ, and thank Him for it.

Something to think/talk/pray about

—"Death is ultimate healing." Is this only a cliché to use when prayers are not answered?

—How does this same statement apply to Jesus' death?

10. The Greatest Miracle of Forgiveness (Easter)

Have you wondered about what the rising from the dead means? When Peter, James, and John were coming with Jesus off the Mount of Transfiguration, Jesus "gave them orders not to tell anyone what they had seen until the Son of Man had risen from the dead. They kept the matter to themselves, discussing what 'rising from the dead' meant" (Mark 9:9). They had reason to. It had not yet happened. They didn't even seriously entertain the idea that it would. But it happened. For nearly 2,000 years now, people have had the opportunity of wondering about this after the fact, after the resurrection took place. Throughout the whole world every Easter, millions wonder about what the rising from the dead means.

One of the primary meanings of the resurrection is forgiveness. The resurrection was forgiveness-centered, forgiveness-oriented. Jesus spoke about it in these terms. He had accomplished some miracles in the presence of people, but then some religious leaders came asking Him to perform more. He referred them directly to the case of Jonah the prophet. Jonah was in the belly of the fish for three days and three nights. When he was delivered safely on the shore, he was sent directly to Nineveh on an errand of forgiveness. He was to preach repentance to them that they might turn from their sins and to God. "The Ninevites believed God. They declared a fast, and all of them, from the greatest to the least, put on sackcloth. . . . When God saw what they did and how they turned from their evil ways, he had compassion and did not bring upon them the destruction he had threatened" (Jonah 3:5, 10). Jesus then said, "One greater than Jonah is here" (Matt. 12:41), indicating that the people should all the more repent and receive forgiveness and restoration. The resurrection of Jesus was the greater event, and a far greater number than the people of Nineveh have heard the proclamation. Jesus said in one of His resurrection appearances: "This is what is written: The Christ will suffer and rise from the dead on the third day, and repentance and forgiveness of sins will be preached in his name to all nations" (Luke 24:46–47). Mark records the Great Commission of Jesus before He ascended: "Go into all the world and preach the good news to all creation. Whoever believes and is baptized will be saved, but whoever does not believe will be condemned" (Mark 16:15–16). The apostle John adds these words about forgiveness: "If you forgive anyone his sins, they are forgiven; if you do not forgive them, they are not forgiven" (John 20:23). What does the rising from the dead mean? It means forgiveness.

Just after the fall of man into sin, a hint of forgiveness was given in these words: "I will put enmity between you and the woman, and between your offspring and hers; he shall crush your head, and you shall strike his heel" (Gen. 3:15). When Jesus died, the serpent struck the heel of the Son. But when Jesus rose again, He crushed the head of the serpent and ended the spread and destructive power of the devil's venom. The resurrection meant forgiveness.

And certainly it involved a miracle. The honesty of the gospel writers at this point adds to the validity of Scripture. If I don't believe something and later find out that it is very true, there is a strong temptation to backtrack and explain or excuse myself for not believing in the first place. There is no such attempt in Scripture to cover up for the unbelief of the disciples when the truth of the resurrection was first presented to them. Listen to some of the words used to describe their first reactions—"perplexed, startled, frightened, didn't believe, troubled, questioning, amazed, trembling, astonishment." The disciples did not spend their time in the upper room thinking, "We have nothing to worry about. Jesus will get up again from the dead. We just have to give Him time." No, they were afraid, worried, disheartened because the end had come. Their Master was no more. All their hopes had been nailed to a cross and killed. Even to think of Him as coming back again would only be wishing for a miracle.

When the miracle did happen, they were not prepared to accept it. The first witnesses couldn't get anyone to take them seriously. The best response was described by saying that they "disbelieved for joy." It was something they wanted to believe, but their common sense told them otherwise. Finally, the Lord's appearance convinced them. Then you have words like "eyes opened, opened their minds to understand, glad, great joy, worshiped Jesus, blessing God!"

Why do you suppose they didn't believe at first? Why did they consider the news of His rising an idle tale? Why, when they saw Him, did they think they saw a ghost (Luke 24:37)? It was because it seemed too good to be true. Death is the end of all things. Death is the final winner in the game of life. Who could think otherwise?

No wonder, then, that they were so overcome with joy when Jesus did appear! This means a smashing victory against a previously undefeated enemy. Also, if the resurrection was really true, then it assured the truth of everything else Jesus had said.

It is still quite a mixed crowd that worships on Easter in our day. Some are just caught up in Easter worship without seriously asking why. Some are disturbed by the thought of resurrection because they are not really convinced of the truth of it. Some are betting on the resurrection, but only as they would bet on a horse race—they aren't really sure whether they will win. Others rejoice because they know He has risen indeed. Many have a touch of all these emotions. Whatever the situation, they sense that they are faced with something unique as they consider the resurrection of Jesus Christ. Either it is a hoax, perpetrated upon more people than any other falsehood, and one that has hung on longer than any other hoax, or else it is simply the greatest miracle—greatest because no one else ever preannounced his victory over death as Jesus did: "We are going up to Jerusalem, and the Son of Man will be betrayed to the chief priests and the teachers of the law. They will condemn him to death and will turn him over to the Gentiles to be mocked and flogged and crucified. On the third day he will be raised to life!" (Matt. 20:18–19).

It was also greatest by Jesus' own judgment. When He spoke about no other sign being given except the sign of Jonah, it was as though the other miracles were not worth mentioning or paled into insignificance when compared with His rising from the dead.

This is also borne out as you survey the rest of the New Testament. We have considered all kinds of miracles attributed to Jesus during His ministry. We started with His birth, then looked at miracles of nature, of healing, of raising the dead, and of casting out demons. In the Book of Hebrews there is passing mention made of "signs, wonders and various miracles" (Heb. 2:4). But except for this, there is no mention of any of the miracles of Jesus by any of the New Testament writers except in the gospels. After the resurrection, no other miracle of Jesus got any publicity. The resurrection makes the headlines. The other miracles are not even found in small print. Everything that needs to be said is said by the resurrection in such a powerful way that the others, in comparison, seem negligible. In Acts, when a replacement for Judas was chosen, the one requirement was that he must be a witness of the resurrection (Acts 1:22). In Peter's preaching, Jesus was proclaimed as the Author of life, whom God raised up, and men were urged to repent and believe that they might be forgiven (Acts 3:15, 19). This was true of all the apostles: "With great power the apostles continued to testify to the resurrection of the Lord Jesus" (Acts 4:33). Paul made powerful reference to the resurrection when he wrote to the Christians at Rome, at Corinth, Galatia, Ephesus, Philippi, Colossae, and Thessalonica. The resurrection was the greatest miracle.

Finally, in the resurrection was the greatest forgiveness. Speaking of the believer's share in the victory, Paul said: "When you were dead in your sins and in the uncircumcision of your sinful nature, God made you alive with Christ. He forgave us all our sins, having canceled the written code, with its regulations, that was against us and that stood opposed to us; he took it away, nailing it to the cross. And having disarmed the powers and authorities, he made a public spectacle of them, triumphing over them by the cross" (Col. 2:13–15). When Jesus died, it was the greatest wrap-up of sin, because He took on Himself the iniquities of the whole world. When He was raised, it was the greatest wrap-up of forgiveness, because the consequence of all those sins was removed.

The resurrection of Jesus Christ was the greatest—the greatest forgiveness and the greatest miracle. And it is also a great miracle when your life or mine is touched and changed by it!

Something to think/talk/pray about

—Easter was God's way of saying to the world: "All is forgiven. Come home!"

—If you were to hang such a sign on the entry to your heart, who would you like to have come by and read it?

11. Miracles—Then and Now: A P.S. (Pentecost Sequel) to This Study of Miracles

Let me tell you about a man who has me somewhat puzzled. I don't know quite what to make of him, and I would be interested in your reaction.

There are many people taking many kinds of trips these days. Some are propelled by rockets to outer space. Others are propelled by drugs to places still farther out. But this man claims that he has been on a trip to heaven. That's right! He is not sure that he went there bodily, but he was there. Yet, he has given only evasive answers to questions regarding the trip.

What was it like? He said, "Indescribable!"

Was it beautiful? "Beyond words!"

What did you see? "I can't begin to tell you!"

Well, what did you hear? "Things I can't repeat!"

I have gotten a little exasperated with this fellow. He can't tell anything about the trip, but still claims he made it. Can you imagine going someplace very special and then not having anything to say about it?

But he has a lot of other stories, too. He tells about special visions and revelations from God, but they cannot be proven either. Don't you think he is just telling stories? Doesn't it sound as though he is letting his imagination run wild? If he does have this special connection with God, you would think it would show more in his life. For example, he has a pretty severe health problem that he cannot cure or control. Perhaps it is a kind of epilepsy, and he has no medicine that will absolutely prevent seizures. These come on him at times when it is most inconvenient and embarrassing, to say the least. And this is only one of his physical problems. He has others from time to time, besides still other troubles and difficulties that are not physical in nature.

If I were this man, I would make a deal with God and trade a few visions for a few healings—you know, one miracle for another. I could get along with less visions if it meant being rid of epilepsy, couldn't you?

Well, what do you think of such a fellow? Doesn't his life seem to be an odd mixture of miracles and no miracles at all? Before we discuss the matter further, read some of this man's own words:

> I must go on boasting. Although there is nothing to be gained, I will go on to visions and revelations from the Lord. I know a man in Christ who fourteen years ago was caught up to the third heaven. Whether it was in the body or out of the body I do not know—God knows. And I know that this man—whether in the body or apart from the body I do not know, but God knows—was caught up to paradise. He heard inexpressible things that man is not permitted to tell. I will boast about a man like that, but I will not boast about myself, except about my weaknesses. Even if I should choose to boast, I would not be a fool, because I would be speaking the truth. But I refrain, so no one will think more of me than what is warranted by what I do or say.
> To keep me from becoming conceited because of these surpassingly great revelations, there was given me a thorn in my flesh, a messenger of Satan, to torment me. Three times I pleaded with the Lord to take it away from me. But he said to me, "My grace is sufficient for you, for my power is made perfect in weakness." Therefore I will boast all the more gladly about my weaknesses, so that Christ's power may rest on me. That is why, for Christ's sake, I delight in weaknesses, in insults, in hardships, in persecutions, in difficulties. For when I am weak, then I am strong.
> I have made a fool of myself, but you drove me to it. I

65

ought to have been commended by you, for I am not in the least inferior to the "super-apostles," even though I am nothing. The things that mark an apostle—signs, wonders and miracles—were done among you with great perseverance (2 Cor. 12:1–12).

His Personal Life

This man, the apostle Paul, had a mixture of miracles and no miracles in his personal life too. There was obviously no shortage of visions, revelations, and messages from God that were miraculous and mysterious in nature. Without being able to rationally explain them, Paul nevertheless testified to their reality.

On the other hand, there were some very unmiraculous factors in his life. He speaks of this mixture of miraculous and unmiraculous in the same sentence: "To keep me from becoming conceited because of these surpassingly great revelations, there was given me a thorn in my flesh, a messenger of Satan, to torment me" (2 Cor. 12:7). This thorn in the flesh was never defined, but it was a physical ailment that was bothersome to Paul, and likely of a conspicuous and embarrassing nature. Some have presumed it to be epilepsy, and so this presumption was developed in our opening remarks about Paul. At any rate, it plagued Paul so that he repeatedly sought the Lord, pleading that this malady be removed. But three times the Lord gave him a quite unmiraculous "No!" as his answer. It was, of course, more than a simple turn-down. There came to Paul a steadying and confident assurance of the Lord's grace and power to sustain and use him in spite of the handicap. Nevertheless, this man of great faith carried in his very body the evidence of divine healing that was desired, but never fulfilled.

His Ministry

A mixture of miracles and no miracles also characterized the ministry of the apostle Paul. We already cited the verse (2 Cor. 12:12) where Paul declared that he had been authenticated by the "things that mark an apostle." The Greek words here for "signs, wonders and miracles" are precisely the ones used to describe the miracles of Jesus in the gospels. These signs and wonders are given the same priority in Paul's ministry as in Jesus' ministry; that is, they were subordinate to the primary task of preaching the Gospel. Paul preached Jesus Christ, and signs and wonders accompanied this preaching. He did not set out to perform miracles and then accompany this performance with a little preaching. In Rom. 15:18–20a Paul writes: "I will not venture to speak of anything except what Christ has accomplished through me in leading the Gentiles to obey God by what I have said and done—by the power of signs and miracles, through the power of the Spirit. So from Jerusalem all the way around to Illyricum, I have fully proclaimed the gospel of Christ. It has always been my ambition to preach the gospel. . . ." Paul's ambition was not to be a great miracle worker, but to be a faithful proclaimer of the Good News of Jesus Christ.

We will now examine some incidents in the ministry of Paul to see in them a strange blend of both the presence of miracles and the absence of them.

Paul met Jesus in a miraculous way (Acts 9). There was a sudden flash of light from heaven that struck him as he approached Damascus. There was a unique conversation with the risen Jesus, heard but not understood by those who were with Paul. There was Paul's sudden loss of sight. There was the special vision to Ananias and the recovery of Paul's sight as Ananias laid hands on Paul and prayed for his healing and filling by the Holy Spirit. (Some think that the thorn in the flesh was a lingering eye problem that began with Paul's three days of blindness. If it was, it would constantly remind Paul of this life-changing encounter with his Lord and of what he had been like without Jesus.) After this miraculous meeting with Jesus, Paul stayed on in Damascus and preached, "proving that Jesus is the Christ" (Acts 9:22). But then a plot against his life developed, and Paul had to get out of town. He was not miraculously whisked away. He left in a most unmiraculous manner, being lowered over the city wall inside a basket!

In the city of Paphos, Paul's preaching was opposed by a magician named Elymas. Paul, filled with the Holy Spirit, rebuked this son of the devil and caused blindness to come upon him. Soon Elymas was stumbling around asking people to lead him by the hand. This miracle climaxed in the conversion of the governor of the island (Acts 13). In contrast to this success, at the next preaching place there developed such intense opposition and persecution against Paul that he simply and unmiraculously had to get out of the area (13:50).

"In Lystra there sat a man crippled in his feet, who was lame from birth and had never walked. He listened to Paul as he was speaking. Paul looked directly at him, saw that he had faith to be healed, and called out, 'Stand up on your feet.' At that, the man jumped up and began to walk" (Acts 14:8–10). This obvious miracle so impressed the Greek crowd that they thought Paul and Barnabas were their gods Zeus and Hermes. Yet soon after this miracle, the Jews organized opposition to Paul, and he was stoned so brutally that they dragged his body outside the city and left him for dead—nothing miraculous about that! But then this nonmiracle is followed by something miraculous. "After the disciples had gathered around him [and likely prayed for his recovery], he got up and went back into the city. The next day [after being nearly stoned to death!] he and Barnabas left for Derbe" (Acts 14:20). Paul's ministry was indeed a strange mixture of the presence of miracles and the absence of them.

Paul's miraculous release from the prison in Philippi is well known. An earthquake shook the prison, opened the doors, and unfastened the prisoners' chains. This event was preceded by an unmiraculous happening in which Paul and Silas were dragged before the city rulers, stripped, and beaten badly with rods. This beating resulted from the wrath of some slave owners who became indignant when Paul miraculously and in the name of Jesus cast an evil spirit of divination out of a slave girl (Acts 16).

In Troas (Acts 20) Paul had many things to say before he left. On the night before his departure he spoke until midnight. A young man couldn't take it. He fell asleep (rather unmiraculously!). Now you can get by with this in a pew, but you don't want to fall asleep on a windowsill three stories up! But Eutychus did, and he fell to the ground and seemed for sure to be dead. Paul went down and ministered to the boy, and he lived (really a miracle). Luke reports that the people were "greatly comforted"—not least Paul, I am sure. After this event Paul returned upstairs and talked until dawn!

Paul gives a wrap-up of his experiences in 2 Cor. 11. For a miracle man, the list includes many difficulties that were not removed or even lightened by any miraculous intervention.

> I have . . . been in prison . . . been flogged . . . been exposed to death again and again. Five times I received from the Jews the forty lashes minus one. Three times I was beaten with rods, once I was stoned, three times I was shipwrecked, I spent a night and a day in the open

sea, I have been constantly on the move. I have been in danger from rivers, in danger from bandits, in danger from my own countrymen, in danger from Gentiles; in danger in the city, in danger in the country, in danger at sea; and in danger from false brothers. I have labored and toiled and have often gone without sleep; I have known hunger and thirst and have often gone without food; I have been cold and naked. Besides everything else, I face the daily pressure of my concern for all the churches (2 Cor. 11:23–28).

We have used the life and ministry of Paul to study the continuation of signs, wonders, and miracles in the early church. On the one hand, there is certainly no solid, unbroken line of miracles that constantly accompanied the preaching or the preachers. There were many times when the message did not get through or was interrupted by the opposition, and the messengers suffered in their attempts to proclaim Jesus.

On the other hand, miracles were prevalent enough so that they were a rather normal and natural part of the church's ministry and the lives of the believers.

Miracles Now

But what of miracles now, in the church of today? Are we to avoid them because they may be confusing or troublesome? If this were so, both Jesus and the early church would have avoided miracles, for they often resulted in misunderstanding and opposition. Or are we to assume that miracles are not meant for our time? Were they somehow restricted as a special impetus to get the church established and going? No, there isn't any evidence that God gave some cutoff date regarding miracles. Scriptural evidence is, in fact, quite to the contrary. The Lord's *promises*, for example, were not restricted to the early church. "I tell you the truth, anyone who has faith in me will do what I have been doing. He will do even greater things than these, because I am going to the Father" (John 14:12). "These signs will accompany those who believe: In my name they will drive out demons; they will speak in new tongues; they will pick up snakes with their hands; and when they drink deadly poison, it will not hurt them at all; they will place their hands on sick people, and they will get well" (Mark 16:17–18). No such promises have any time limit attached to them.

Since miracles attested to the presence of the Lord, it is important to note whether there is any indication of a diminished *presence* of God in the church today. Scripture does not say so. "I am with you *always*, to the very end of the age" (Matt. 28:20). "I will ask the Father, and he will give you another Counselor to be with you *forever*" (John 14:16). God's presence with His people is current, is now, is today. He has never been satisfied to be a God of the past, and among the evidences of His presence in the world have always been signs and wonders and miracles.

What is true of His promises and presence is also true of His *power*. If a power company is going to have a cutoff, its customers are generally warned in advance. But there is no such warning to the church from God in Scripture. The task of the church is to witness, and power is assured for the task. "You are witnesses of these things. I am going to send you what my Father has promised; but stay in the city, until you have been clothed with power from on high" (Luke 24:48–49). "You will receive power when the Holy Spirit comes on you; and you will be my witnesses" (Acts 1:8). It was the testimony of the early church that the Lord kept His promises, that He was present with them, and that the Holy Spirit's power put exclamation points behind the message of the Gospel. "Our gospel came to you not simply with words, but also with power, with the Holy Spirit" (1 Thess. 1:5). "My message and my preaching were not with wise and persuasive words, but with a demonstration of the Spirit's power" (1 Cor. 2:4). "This [message of] salvation, which was first announced by the Lord, was confirmed to us by those who heard him. God also testified to it by signs, wonders and various miracles, and gifts of the Holy Spirit distributed according to his will" (Heb. 2:3–4).

God has not run out on His promises. God has not run off with His presence. God has not run out of power. The problem is that we do not plug into His power as we should. God's people today are not appropriating His power. Miracles never have taken place when an uncommitted church sits back and expects to be entertained by miracles. But exciting things do happen when the church gets busy with the task of proclaiming Christ. Signs and wonders accompanied the preaching of Jesus Christ as Lord, and still do. Signs and wonders accompanied the believing and receiving of Him as Savior, and still do.

This is the Holy Spirit's day in the church. It has been so since Pentecost. The *task of witnessing* roots in Him. "When the

Counselor comes, whom I will send to you from the Father, the Spirit of truth who goes out from the Father, he will testify about me. And you also must testify, for you have been with me from the beginning" (John 15:26–27). The *response* of faith *to this witness* is also the Spirit's doing. "No one can say, 'Jesus is Lord,' except by the Holy Spirit" (1 Cor. 12:3). And, finally, *signs, wonders, and miracles accompanying this witness* are the domain of the Holy Spirit.

He exercises this domain in three ways. First, the Holy Spirit empowers us to expect God's miraculous working. Paul reminded Timothy that "God did not give us a spirit of timidity, but a spirit of power" (2 Tim. 1:7). We tend to pray for the sick timidly and carefully in such a way that we guard our reputation and God's reputation in the event that no healing takes place! It is the Holy Spirit who makes us bold enough to ask relief for a person's most pressing need. Or we cautiously discuss or diagnose emotional and spiritual hang-ups lest we offend a person in our evaluation of his problem. The Holy Spirit does not seek to be offensive, but He does empower us to label the opposition and implore God's help, "for our struggle is not against flesh and blood, but against the rulers, against the authorities, against the powers of this dark world and against the spiritual forces of evil in the heavenly realms" (Eph. 6:12).

Expecting a miracle does not bring it about, but not expecting a miracle can prevent it. James' words apply here: "You do not have, because you do not ask God" (4:2). There is quite a difference between a healthy trust that all things are possible with God, and a conviction that it is our responsibility not to assign God any task too great for Him! As the Holy Spirit empowers us to expect God's powerful action, He is also equipping us to *experience* it. When you study the signs, wonders, and miracles of Jesus and of the early disciples, you sense an atmosphere of expectancy rather than surprise. This is the kind of trustful optimism we need in the church today.

A third work of the Holy Spirit in the area of miracles is that He *enlightens* us to see miracles in their proper perspective. We have generally defined a miracle as "an act or happening in the material or physical sphere that apparently departs from the laws of nature or goes beyond what is known concerning these laws." Because a miracle is "unusual," we tend to label it "exceptional." But the Holy Spirit is the Spirit of truth, and He causes us to revel in the "natural" of God's order even more than in the "unnatural" interference with that order. For example, an instantaneous healing is a blessing, but natural and continual good health is a greater blessing. The stilling of a storm is helpful, but days of regular sunshine and rain are more beneficial. We would call it a miracle if the sun stood still for an hour, but isn't it most wonderful that it continues its faithful, scheduled rising and setting? To be raised from the dead is magnificent, but for life to go on uninterrupted by death is better yet, and the promise of eternal life is best of all. To be freed from an evil spirit is a cleansing, but to know total forgiveness in Jesus is to be made really clean.

God grant His church today an ambition to be spent in proclaiming Jesus, a contentment that enhances the proclamation, and an excitement as mighty works punctuate it.

Something to think/talk/pray about

—In what ways do you identify with Paul as he lived with and without miracles?

—"Expecting a miracle does not bring it about, but not expecting a miracle may prevent it." Is this relevant to any of your experiences?

—Make a list of blessings that are "naturally" yours.